GET IT DONE ON TIME!

A CRITICAL CHAIN PROJECT MANAGEMENT/THEORY OF CONSTRAINTS NOVEL

Eric Bergland

apress®

Get it Done On Time! A Critical Chain Project Management/Theory of Constraints Novel

Eric Bergland
Redwood City, California
USA

ISBN-13 (pbk): 978-1-4842-1859-4   ISBN-13 (electronic): 978-1-4842-1860-0
DOI 10.1007/978-1-4842-1860-0

Library of Congress Control Number: 2016941935

Copyright © 2016 by Eric Bergland

This work is subject to copyright. All rights are reserved by the Publisher, whether the whole or part of the material is concerned, specifically the rights of translation, reprinting, reuse of illustrations, recitation, broadcasting, reproduction on microfilms or in any other physical way, and transmission or information storage and retrieval, electronic adaptation, computer software, or by similar or dissimilar methodology now known or hereafter developed. Exempted from this legal reservation are brief excerpts in connection with reviews or scholarly analysis or material supplied specifically for the purpose of being entered and executed on a computer system, for exclusive use by the purchaser of the work. Duplication of this publication or parts thereof is permitted only under the provisions of the Copyright Law of the Publisher's location, in its current version, and permission for use must always be obtained from Springer. Permissions for use may be obtained through RightsLink at the Copyright Clearance Center. Violations are liable to prosecution under the respective Copyright Law.

Trademarked names, logos, and images may appear in this book. Rather than use a trademark symbol with every occurrence of a trademarked name, logo, or image we use the names, logos, and images only in an editorial fashion and to the benefit of the trademark owner, with no intention of infringement of the trademark.

The use in this publication of trade names, trademarks, service marks, and similar terms, even if they are not identified as such, is not to be taken as an expression of opinion as to whether or not they are subject to proprietary rights.

While the advice and information in this book are believed to be true and accurate at the date of publication, neither the authors nor the editors nor the publisher can accept any legal responsibility for any errors or omissions that may be made. The publisher makes no warranty, express or implied, with respect to the material contained herein.

    Managing Director: Welmoed Spahr
    Lead Editor: Jeffrey Pepper
    Technical Reviewer: Suzan Bergland
    Editorial Board: Steve Anglin, Pramila Balan, Louise Corrigan, Jonathan Gennick,
        Robert Hutchinson, Celestin Suresh John, Michelle Lowman, James Markham,
        Susan McDermott, Matthew Moodie, Jeffrey Pepper, Douglas Pundick,
        Ben Renow-Clarke, Gwenan Spearing
    Coordinating Editor: Mark Powers
    Compositor: SPi Global
    Indexer: SPi Global
    Artist: SPi Global

Distributed to the book trade worldwide by Springer Science+Business Media New York, 233 Spring Street, 6th Floor, New York, NY 10013. Phone 1-800-SPRINGER, fax (201) 348-4505, e-mail orders-ny@springer-sbm.com, or visit www.springeronline.com. Apress Media, LLC is a California LLC and the sole member (owner) is Springer Science + Business Media Finance Inc (SSBM Finance Inc). SSBM Finance Inc is a **Delaware** corporation.

For information on translations, please e-mail rights@apress.com, or visit www.apress.com.

Apress and friends of ED books may be purchased in bulk for academic, corporate, or promotional use. eBook versions and licenses are also available for most titles. For more information, reference our Special Bulk Sales–eBook Licensing web page at www.apress.com/bulk-sales.

Any source code or other supplementary materials referenced by the author in this text are available to readers at www.apress.com/9781484217085. For detailed information about how to locate your book's source code, go to www.apress.com/source-code/. Readers can also access source code at SpringerLink in the Supplementary Material section for each chapter.

Printed on acid-free paper

Contents

About the Author... v
About the Technical Reviewer................................... vii
Acknowledgments ix
Preface.. xi

Chapter 1:   Introductions 1
Chapter 2:   High-Level Critical Chain Overview................... 5
Chapter 3:   Factors for Successful Implementations 25
Chapter 4:   How Does the Critical Chain Solution Work?........... 37
Chapter 5:   Championing Ideas.................................... 57
Chapter 6:   High-Level Implementation Steps 77
Chapter 7:   Using Ambitious Targets to Handle Past Issues........ 93
Chapter 8:   Individual Buy-In.................................... 107
Chapter 9:   Almost 129
Chapter 10: Board Room Meeting................................... 135
Appendix A: 145

Index 189

About the Author

Eric Bergland has been in software product development for over 20 years working as a software engineer, product manager, and project and program manager. Eric completed a computer science degree from Ithaca College and his master's degree in telecommunications from the University of Pittsburgh. He started his TOC journey in 1993 with the Goldratt Institute's Odyssey college program lead by Dr. Eli Goldratt. Eric also worked for the Goldratt Institute and went through its Academy training program learning the Critical Chain project management solutions, Theory of Constraints problem solving model, Management Skills Workshop day-to-day tools, replenishment distribution solution, and drum-buffer-rope manufacturing solutions. He has applied his Theory of Constraints and Critical Chain knowledge in a variety of organizations and enjoys sharing his experiences with TOC in the stories collected here.

About the Technical Reviewer

Suzan Bergland has worked with numerous organizations to help them improve their bottom-line results and to create a sustainable competitive advantage. In 2013 she retired from AGI-Goldratt Institute after serving as a partner and as president of the North American group. She is a founder and lifetime member of the Theory of Constraints International Certification Organization (TOCICO) and holds all six TOCICO certifications (Supply Chain Logistics, Thinking Process, Holistic Strategy, Project Management, Finance, and Measures and Fundamentals). Suzan is coauthor of the book *VELOCITY–Combining Lean, Six Sigma, and the Theory of Constraints to Achieve Breakthrough Performance,* published by Simon & Schuster. Suzan holds a bachelor's degree from Furman University, a master's degree from Converse College, and a master's degree in quality management from Loyola University in New Orleans.

Acknowledgments

I would like to thank the Goldratt Institute, where I first learned about the Theory of Constraints, Eli Goldratt, who created the Theory of Constraints methodology, and the TOC community. Thanks also to Jeff, Mark, Matt, and the Apress team for their support and publishing expertise. I would also like to thank Suzan Bergland for sharing her insights and expertise and my family (Frances, Spencer, and Ryan) for their love and support.

Preface

This book is based on actual real-world experiences and project management tools. It covers a variety of project management, Critical Chain, Theory of Constraints, and organizational adoption (buy-in) situations and concepts. It is designed to provide a fun, entertaining, and comprehensive way to learn these concepts, trigger discussions, and give you some ideas of what to look for in your organization.

If you interested in the Theory of Constraints and Critical Chain, this book will provide a great overview of the various concepts, how they can be implemented in real-world situations, and the buy-in required when putting these (or any) project management tools into place.

If you are interested in learning more about project management and are familiar with other tools and techniques, you should find the examples and situations in the stories familiar and compelling. You should be able to see common project management challenges, look at what tools you are familiar with and how they could apply, and then see how they compare or complement the tools and approaches the characters use to implement, gain adoption, and gain success in your organization.

To help with understanding the concepts introduced in each chapter, a series of concept summaries and optional discussion questions are provided in the appendix.

Note At the end of some chapters, I provide Current Reality Tree (CRT) and Future Reality Tree (FRT) diagrams. These will be explained fully in the relevant chapters. However, as key issues and benefits are raised in the story, they will be tagged with [crt #] or [frt #] to help you connect them with items captured and summarized in the CRT and FRT. In other words, [crt #] and [frt #] are references to items in the CRT and FRT, respectively.

Like any field, Critical Chain and the Theory of Constraints (TOC) is ever evolving and new ideas, concepts, understandings, and refinements are always being developed. To learn the latest information and more about TOC, TOC solutions including Critical Chain, TOC conferences, results, and testimonials, consider the following:

- The Goldratt Institute (www.goldratt.com), which is the birthplace of TOC.
- The Theory of Constraints International Certification Organization (www.tocico.org).

CHAPTER 1

Introductions

Tim sat watching as all of LivingTV Interactive's employees slowly gathered into the company's atrium to hear the CEO's latest pep talk.

"We have a great product. We delivered a great service..," the CEO started out. Then it turned, "We were just before our time. We could not build the market fast enough. We are being forced to close our doors."

Everyone looked around shocked. Everyone knew things had been challenging over the last year, but they did not realize they were this bad, or that they would end this suddenly.

LivingTV

LivingTV had started out small with wild ideas and big dreams. They built a prototype out of blood and sweat, pouring in hours of overtime to steadily growing the company's technology. Then a few years later came the big push to expand. Go public—launch a new technology and make everyone millionaires. As part of this big expansion they leased out a building four times their current size. They pushed to build up reserves of venture capital and major investment money. They grew from 40 to 150 employees. But, they could not develop the market fast enough. They could not get the new technology out soon enough. They were unable to grow the revenues as quickly as they had expanded the company and counter the resulting growth in expenses. Dreams are good but expanding quickly past your capabilities can turn out to be very, very fatal.

Electronic supplementary material The online version of this chapter (doi:10.1007/978-1-4842-1860-0_1) contains supplementary material, which is available to authorized users.

© Eric Bergland 2016
E. Bergland, *Get it Done On Time!*, DOI 10.1007/978-1-4842-1860-0_1

Chapter 1 | Introductions

The company was gone; left to a handful of patents for its investors and lawyers to fight over. Tim started to promote the Theory of Constraints (TOC) at LivingTV. But too little, too late. Now, like 149 others, Tim too had to figure out what was next. Do some engineering work? Maybe consulting? Probably best to ponder his next steps over a cup of coffee at his favorite coffee shop.

Tim and Randal Reconnect

"TIM!!! Hey Tim!!" Tim looks around and tries to shake the cobwebs out of his head. Someone is yelling across what used to be a quiet coffee shop disturbing Tim and multiple patrons in the process. It is Randal, an old college buddy Tim has not seen in years. He has aged a bit, is dressed to the hilt in a fancy suit, and is quickly advancing toward Tim's table.

"TIM!! What are you up to buddy?" Randal says, full of zeal and vigor.

"Not too much at the moment Randal; just contemplating my options," Tim responds somewhat lethargically.

"Options! So how soon is your company going public? Will you be able to cash them out pretty soon or are you in the lock-out period?"

"Well," Tim says, wanting to get this over with, "my options started out at $12 per share."

"Not too bad; so what are they worth now? Have they grown in value?"

"Well, the company just folded a few hours ago," Tim responds, "so I'm figuring they're worthless now. But I could possibly use them for wallpaper," he says, half joking. "What I was really contemplating were my job options."

"Oh Tim! I am very sorry to hear that. No worries, though. You're good. I'm sure you will figure out something in no time."

"So how about you, Randal?" says Tim, anxious to change the topic.

"I worked at a few companies here and there, building up my marketing skills over the last few years since we last saw each other. Right now I'm very excited about finishing up my executive marketing MBA. I'm hoping it will give me a chance to move up the corporate ladder a bit. As part of the MBA graduation requirement, I have an internship at a software start-up.

"What is the new software start-up like?" The software part catches Tim's interest.

"The software company has been around for a few years and they are getting ready to launch their latest line of products. The company has made it through several rounds of funding. We just need to get some of our new products out to a few key customers and we're good to go. I even get some of the pre-IPO stock as part of my internship contract. How about you, Tim? Last we talked, you were looking into project management consulting."

"Correct. I learned about the Critical Chain project management solution and I was trying to use it to help LivingTV deliver its projects more quickly and reliably."

"Interesting," Randal says, thinking about some of the issues he heard during his internship, "I might want to hear a bit more about that."

"I was also able to learn a great set of TOC tools."

"TOC as in Table of Contents?" Randal says, staring strangely at Tim.

"No, no. TOC as in Theory of Constraints. It is a great set of general problem-solving tools that you can use to look at the organization as a whole, identify areas to focus on, and drive overall improvements."

"That part sounds a bit involved," Randal says, his eyes glazing over.

"It can be an important step. The TOC analysis can help ensure the Critical Chain implementation's success. In fact, the TOC analysis can help focus teams on any improvement effort from Critical Chain, Scrum, Agile, new technology deployments, and so on."

Randal looks a bit unconvinced. Then, looking down at his watch, he says, "Crap, late again. Tim I have to head off to an exec strategy meeting. Maybe we can meet here Monday and you can tell me a bit more about Critical Chain and meeting deadlines? Same time? I'll call you just before to confirm."

"Ahh…sure," Tim says hesitantly. "My schedule seems to be pretty open."

CHAPTER 2

High-Level Critical Chain Overview

Tim sits idly in his favorite café, looking repeatedly at his watch. He's 15 minutes late. Don't marketing guys have any concept of time, he thinks, half joking to himself. Finally he sees Randal's BMW drive into the packed parking lot and pull into an empty handicap spot. Randal turns off the car and then casually places a temporary handicap placard on his rear view mirror and quickly strides into the cafe.

"Hi Randal, good to see you. I saw the handicap placard. Are you doing okay?" Tim asks, somewhat concerned and curious.

"Hi Tim. Thank you for asking. I'm doing alright. I thrashed my back last week playing tennis; couldn't walk a damn. It expires next week. I figured I just might as well take advantage of it while I still can."

Tim thought back to the last time he had worked with Randal. Tim had always been an altruistic spirit of the rules, try-and-make-a-better-system kind of guy, where Randal had been much more practical, making the most of the rules he was given. "I'm glad your back is doing better," Tim replies. "So Randal, over the phone you said you wanted to learn a bit more about Critical Chain?"

© Eric Bergland 2016
E. Bergland, *Get it Done On Time!*, DOI 10.1007/978-1-4842-1860-0_2

"Correct Tim. I was hoping you could give me a high-level explanation and I wanted to see if it was something our engineering team could use. I did some checking and heard that they talked about Critical Chain, but I don't think they got very far. I wanted to hear about your experience and if it was something that you found useful."

Tim thinks to himself briefly. In the past, he tried to provide lots of project management details to someone who was more business focused. It only succeeded in confusing the person rather than helping them understand. Always best to start high level and then go into details as needed. "Sure Randal, I'll walk you through a quick introduction. If you want more details, just let me know. Does that work for you?"

"Sure Tim, fire away."

"Critical Chain is a Theory of Constraints solution that addresses the common problems found in project management so we can better plan, manage, and be more successful with projects. Randal, are you familiar with traditional scheduling and Critical Path?"

"Just the basics, Tim. You build out an overall schedule by looking at defining all of the tasks and work involved and their inter-connections. Then you identify the Critical Path, which is the longest sequence of tasks needed to complete the project. From there, you focus your efforts on managing the Critical Path. I've seen Gary, the engineering manager, run a few schedule building sessions."

"So one of the first steps in the Critical Chain is to be sure that your resources are leveled."

"Resource what?"

"Resource leveled. It is a function within the scheduling tool that makes sure that you do not schedule more than one task to a resource at a time. Think of it this way. If I asked you to go to one customer tradeshow the first week of June *and* I asked you to fly to Florida to support a customer demo the same week…"

"It would be impossible to do, Tim."

"Exactly. So we resolve resource contention or level the work so we're not asking resources to do more than one full time task at a time."

"Sure, put that way, it sounds like a very good idea."

"Second, Critical Chain is very focused on managing variability—any time a task might finish later or sooner than expected. Simply put, if there were never any delays in schedules then project management would be a snap. Since there are always delays and we don't know where or when, Critical Chain helps us manage this variability."

"How?"

"So Critical Chain focuses on trying to reduce behaviors that cause delays and sets up buffers to absorb and manage delays. It also focuses less on individual deadlines and more on the overall deadline, also known as the project due date."

"Tim, I know Gary gets all bent out of shape when resources are late and the project starts to run late. So is Critical Chain just setting up more milestones and is less focused on the tasks?"

"Not quite, Randal. Think of it this way. If every task was late but the project still delivered on time, the project would be a success. At the same time, if every task was on time, but the project was still late it would be not be a success."

"True Tim, but not realistic."

"But true in the sense that at the end of the day we care the most about the overall project deadline. So if the schedule was set up in a way that task delays could be absorbed by an overall buffer that protected the overall deadline—the thing we care about the most—this would be of value."

"I guess, Tim. We definitely have issues hitting our overall deadlines. So anything to better protect them would be of value. I would have to think a bit more about this and more likely need to pull Gary in. So you said Critical Chain was part of the Theory of Constraints. Like a physics theory or something?"

"So the *Theory of Constraints* (TOC for short) is a general problem-solving model that can be applied to a variety of environments, but it has one fundamental concept. In looking at any kind of system such as project management, manufacturing, or distribution, it implies that if you look in the right way and hard enough you will find that there is one thing, one constraint, that limits the overall system. So if you focus improvement efforts on this one area, the whole system will benefit and the bottom line of the organization will improve."

"Hmm…Tim, like you said, it sounds a rather bit academic and theoretical. Is it really true?

"Well, let's go back to Critical Chain. TOC looked at all of the common project management issues, looked at how they were interconnected, and what were the root issues driving them. It then focused building a solution to address these issues. For example, one of the biggest issues with traditional schedules is that once you are late there is not an inherent system to recover. So that is why Critical Chain focuses so much on reducing variability (behaviors and level loading) and managing it (buffers). The better you can manage variability (one possible constraint) the more likely the overall project (system) will succeed."

"So TOC was used to create Critical Chain?"

"Correct. And it can be used to help with the implementation of Critical Chain."

"Hmm. Interesting thoughts Tim," Randal turns to his coffee and takes a few sips. "So, that was a good text book background do you have something more real world you can share with me? So it's a project management system. So what is the marketing pitch? Which customer pain points does it address? What are the benefits? What is the value? Give me some real-world examples."

Critical Chain Issues, Benefits, and Sample Results

Tim pauses for a moment and collects his thoughts. "Sure Randal. So Critical Chain helps us address several common project management *issues* that happen in a variety of project management environments. Some of the most common ones are:

- Projects miss critical deadlines and market opportunities [crt 25]
- We cut too many key features to make deadlines [crt 19]
- Our products are not competitive enough (due to slow project turnaround, missing deadlines, and cutting key features) [crt 23]
- There is too much resource burn-out and turnover [crt 14]
- We go over budget due to project overruns and do not make expected revenues for our product lines [crt 26]
- There are internal projects that fight over shared resources [crt 18]

"That's quite a list, Tim. Missing deadlines, cutting features, and being competitive all make sense to me. We would have to talk with Gary about resource burn-out and struggles. Give me some more time and I could work with Gary and probably come up with a few more items to expand your list."

"True, these are the key issues. Depending on the organization, some of these issues will stand out more than others or be phrased slightly differently."

"So, Tim, let me give you a marketing tip. It's great that Critical Chain can help address all of those issues. The real question is if one of those issues is really critical and more significant than the others, then I am very likely to pay big bucks to fix it. In other words, what are the customer's biggest pain points?"

Get it Done On Time!

"Okay…" feeling a bit odd to be lectured by Randal, "So Randal, from the list of issues I just went over, what really stands out to you?"

"Great question Tim! For us, hitting the major deadlines is the single most important factor. If we miss the deadlines, we delay our funding. Cutting features and resource burn-out are some factors. But far and beyond everything is about hitting the deadlines."

"And Randal, what happens if you consistently miss schedules to the point that you continue to lose funding?"

"Well in that unlikely case it happens enough, it is likely the company could eventually run out of money and fold shortly thereafter [crt 28]. Which would be bad. But hey I'm a marketing consultant and missing schedules would be engineering's fault."

"And how well is engineering holding up meeting schedules?"

"They're okay, but as the company is ramping up, so does the work, the deadlines, and the pressure. I guess, thinking more about it, the delays are likely to get worse and worse pretty soon."

"And if the company folds soon, what happens to your MBA internship?" Tim asks, building on the discussion.

"My internship goes away. Oh crap! That means I would not be able to close out the internship requirement for my MBA and I could be held back at least a year!"

"And the company's health and employees could be at risk too?" Tim inquires, trying to get Randal to think beyond just his own interests.

"Yeah, yeah, that too," Randal says a bit disheartened.

"Okay, Randal, as you say, I think we have successfully found the company's, as well as your personal, biggest pain point, and why we need to look at improving the company's project management."

"Yeah, I'll say. I thought being in marketing and an intern, I was safe. I guess it's a bit more complicated than I thought."

"So we covered the common project management issues. Being a bit more hopeful, let us talk about some of the common Critical Chain benefits. They include:

- On-time delivery of products significantly improves [frt 8]
- You are able to complete projects much faster [frt 8]
- Hidden or misused resource capacity is identified [frt 12]
- The company and its products are more competitive [frt 14]
- The company is more profitable [frt 20]"

"That seems like a reasonable list, Tim."

Taking a cue from Randal's earlier comment, Tim asks, "So what benefits stand out to you the most, Randal?"

"Well Tim, as I said before, right now it's critical to get reliable, consistent, on-time delivery. Not only is it important for the survivability of the company, but also for our long-term profitability."

"So we have identified your key issue as well as the key benefit to focus on and help move the company forward with Critical Chain," states Tim.

"Um, not quite Tim. The issues and benefits sound nice and all. But I have heard these same benefits time and time again claimed by other project management vendors and solutions. I need to know this is real. Show me proven results. And tell me without confusing me why this Critical Chain can really deliver these results. Then I might be a bit more motivated and convinced."

"Okay, okay, Randal," Tim concedes, a bit surprised at the push back. "Give me a bit more time and I can address all of your questions."

"Wouldn't want to make it too easy for you Tim," Randal says with a friendly smile.

"Well Randal, you are in luck. I happen to have a few examples with me." Tim then proceeds to pulls out a folder of printed documents. "So every company and circumstance is unique, but what you can see here are some of the exceptional results that some companies have been able to achieve from a variety of different Critical Chain providers."

Avraham Goldratt Institute (AGI)

Using their experience and Critical Chain, they have the following customer results (see www.goldratt.com) (2.3):

- Seagate brought the first 15,000 rpm disc to market ahead of competition, causing all competition to pull out of the market.

- Harris Semiconductor used Critical Chain to manage construction of its $250 million wafer fabrication plant, completing it in just 13 months where the historic average was 54 months.

- Lucent Technologies tripled its development project capacity (5 to 17), reduced its new product introduction interval by 50%, and completed 100% of their projects ahead of time.

Goldratt Marketing Group

www.toc-goldratt.com has a TOC reference bank of results that includes (2.4):

- eIRCOM telecommunications improved due date performance from 40% to 90% and significantly reduced lead times.

Realization

Realization lists several customer summaries, brief case studies, and customer videos at http://www.realization.com (2.6).

High Tech New Product Development. HP Digital Camera Group:

- Before: Six cameras launched in 2004. One camera launched in the spring window. One out of six cameras launched on time.
- After: 15 cameras launched in 2005, with 25% lower R&D expenses. Seven cameras launched in their spring window. All 15 cameras launched on time.

Aircraft Repair and Overhaul. US Air Force, Warner Robins Air Logistics Center, C17 Production Line:

- Before: Throughput of 178 hours per aircraft per day. Turnaround time 46-180 days. Mechanic output 3.6 hours per day.
- After: 25% increase in throughput. Turnaround time reduced to 37-121 days. Mechanic output increased to 4.75 hours per day. 40% overtime reduction.

ProChain

ProChain lists several customer success stories as well at http://www.prochain.com (2.7). Clients have experienced:

- 20-50% reduction in actual execution of projects
- 30-60% increase in productivity
- 50-200% increase in project throughput
- Return on investments ratio greater than 100:1
- Significant improvement in quality of life
- Stable and continuous process improvement

Chapter 2 | High-Level Critical Chain Overview

There is also an example of Habitat for Humanity using Critical Chain scheduling to set a new world record building a four bedroom house in 3 hours, 44 minutes, and 59 seconds. (2.8)

"So Tim, these are some very compelling results. Can I expect these same results in my organization?"

"That is a great question, Randal. It depends on your individual circumstances. In implementing Critical Chain, some organizations have found huge opportunities where they can significantly improve their operations. Other companies have found significant improvements, but not as dramatic as these. As we walk through better understanding Critical Chain as well as how your organization works, we can highlight the opportunities and potential impacts of implementing Critical Chain."

"Okay, Tim, that makes sense. These results look promising. Individual results may vary. So tell me how can Critical Chain really deliver?"

Key Parts of Critical Chain

"So, as you asked Randal, how does Critical Chain get these results? Some of the key parts include:

- Project buffers to better manage task variability [frt 1]
- Reducing bad multi-tasking to find hidden and misused resource capacity [frt 1]
- Setting goals and building schedules back to front [frt 1]
- Organizational analysis (TOC TP) to better understand the overall project environment (creating the CRT and FRT)

"Whoa, Tim, this is a little terminology heavy and some of these do not make sense to me. I'm just a simple marketing guy." Randal says, raising his hands up and smiling. "Can you give me a high-level explanation of these and then we can possibly dig into them in more detail with Gary?"

"Sure, Randal."

Project Buffers to Better Manage Variability

"So Randal, as I asked before, what is the key issue in project management?"

"Managing project risks effectively, hitting deadlines, staffing, managing scope, and building the right product all come to mind, Tim."

"Those are all good Randal, but as I noted before, one key thing to look at is *variability*."

"Sure Tim, I have some familiarity with variability. It is what Gary talks about all the time when his team misses a deadline. He talks about there being more work involved than originally expected, that additional scope and requirements were added, resources were not available, tasks took longer than expected, and worse project disasters happened that can totally sink a project."

"True and when we originally build a schedule, how do they take into account this variability?"

"Well of course Gary does. Kinda… Well, maybe not exactly. He asks the engineers for their estimates, he ties everything together, and then we call it a schedule. Well, actually an initial estimate. Then management looks at the estimate and starts cutting out time. Then we end up with something that management feels is aggressive and somewhat realistic and something that engineering doesn't scream too excessively about."

"And how often do you meet these schedules, Randal?"

"The original schedule or the latest version of the revised schedule?"

"The original." asks Tim.

"Well Tim, in general, not at all or at least never consistently. Engineering hits the typical unexpected and unplanned issues—they're juggling multiple projects, complain about being stretched out and understaffed. They ask for more time; sometimes we replan and give them more time, and even then they're likely to miss it. If we don't give them more time, they're likely to push out anyway or cut major features."

"So Randal, does it look like this process is working for you in the long run?"

"Well… No, not really"

Tim draws the following diagram.

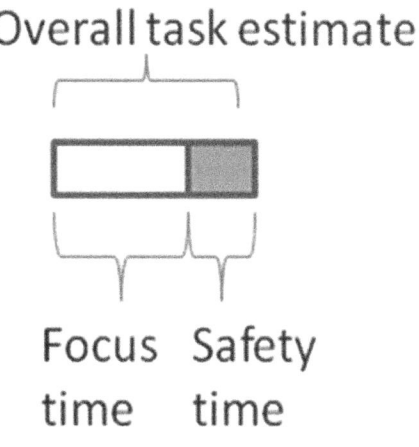

Chapter 2 | High-Level Critical Chain Overview

"So, Critical Chain sets up a formal system to better manage project variability. When an engineer estimates a task, there can be two sets of time. *Focused time* is the ideal time the task would take if the engineer just worked on that one task with no problems and no interruptions. *Safety time* is the padding the engineer adds to that focused time estimate to take into account possible issues, such as the other work they are doing, paranoia, etc. For Critical Chain, we build the schedule based on the focused time and aggregate the safety time from all tasks to create a project buffer at the end of the project [frt 1]."

"So Tim, is this similar to using aggressive task estimates and then putting a management buffer at the end of the project since you figure they will run late?"

Tim then draws the following diagram.

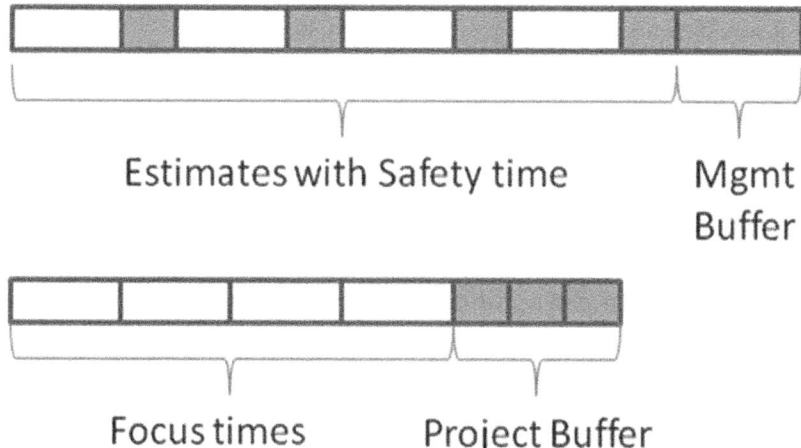

"Close, but there are some fundamental differences. A management buffer is simply adding more time to a schedule that includes safety time in it. So you are adding a management buffer to an engineering task buffered schedule. This stretches out the schedule even more. Critical Chain uses aggressive focused times and the project buffer at the end of the project is more strategic and effective. In addition, you define strategies to manage this buffer and trigger actions if the buffer is being consumed too quickly too soon, so there is more to it than a management buffer at the end of a schedule. Since the project buffer is more strategic than buffering each task, we find that we can often use less time and still get good protection against delays. To help effectively manage the project time, we also focus on behaviors to reduce bad multi-tasking and look at ways to more rigorously build the schedule, which leads us to our next two items."

"Okay, Tim that sounds a bit more developed than what we are currently using." I will have to bring in Gary and see what he thinks."

Reducing Bad Multi-Tasking to Find Hidden and Misused Resource Capacity

"So Randal, have you ever driven on Highway 101 during lunch time?"

"Sure, it's a breeze; I can often finish my work commute in 20 minutes or so."

"And Randal, during the 5:00 rush hour, how long is your commute?"

"Horrendous. It can take up to an hour; worse if there is an accident."

"So your commute time can actually triple, but the distance from work to your house never changed."

"Correct."

"So that is what we look for with *bad multi-tasking*. A highway has a certain capacity of cars it can handle. When there are not a lot of cars, traffic can flow rather quickly and just adding more cars has minimal effect. But once you start to swamp the road's capacity, all the cars slow down more and more. The distance people have to drive has not changed, just the rate at which they can travel. The same is true with assigning projects to resources and to organizations. At a minimal point, we can just assign a handful of projects and they get done quickly—this is a reasonable amount of multi-tasking. But when we assign too many projects and all of them need to get done, the work starts to slow down more and more. This is a big sign of bad multi-tasking, where work and the time to finish our projects is getting more and more stretched out."

"Interesting, Tim. Our engineers are getting busier and busier. And it certainly seems like they are getting overworked and are slowing down; in fact the more work we add, the more it just piles up and we have to just sit and wait for them to even get to it."

"This is exactly what we look for in trying to address this area. Give resources clear priorities; focusing resources on key projects versus spreading them out on multiple projects; drive the resources on focused time so they focus on the key task; minimize set up and set down time; encourage quick hand-offs when tasks are completed; and don't punish resources for finishing early or for when their tasks take longer than the focused time and consume some of the project buffer."

"This is an interesting observation, Tim. We'll have to go into this one a bit more when Gary is here."

"Fair enough."

"So Tim, project buffers and reducing bad multi-tasking are the key differences that Critical Chain has?"

"Two main differences, but let me share the last two major differences as well."

Setting Goals and Building Schedules (Back to Front)

"So Randal, there are a variety of approaches to building a project schedule. The one key thing I have seen is that true dependencies are not always called out."

"Okay..." Randal responds a bit hesitantly.

"In building the schedule, back to front, we first outline the goal of the project. From there, we work backward, in regard to what is essential to accomplish that goal. This helps us identify what is critical and confirm we have captured the true dependencies."

"Tim, that kinda makes sense, but do you have a real example that I can better relate to?"

"Sure, let me give you my interpretation of one example I have seen. At the time, the industry average for building a semiconductor plant was 54 months. This was based on building the facility, installing the machines, and then training the employees. All of these areas must be operational before revenues from the project would be realized. It was a very involved and linear process. Using Critical Chain, Harris Semiconductor identified and challenged these assumptions. That, in turn, allowed them to significantly compress their entire schedule. They completed an industry average task of 54 months in 13 months. Think three and half years of additional revenue!"

"This example seems to be too good to be true, Tim. From what little I understand, semiconductor plants are extremely complex and involve very technical and experienced people to build them. And people have been building them for years. What could the whole industry miss that Harris didn't?"

"Using Critical Chain, Harris was able to challenge the conventional wisdom. The convention was to break the overall project into distinct and manageable sub-projects. You have one project and team build the building and once it was done then you had another project and team install the machines and only then you hired and staffed the building. One key step of Critical Chain and setting the goal of the project is to drive the project all the way to *throughput*, or more specifically when the plant would generate revenue."

"You are losing me here, Tim. Why was one large project going to revenue be any better than the multiple sub-projects?"

"It changed the mindset. Instead of just focusing on the sub-project goal of finishing the building, the team was able to focus on how to get the plant operational and generating income. It drove them to think about several key and previously assumed questions. Did you really have to finish the entire building or just key parts before installing the machines? Did you really have to install all the machines before you could start hiring and training? Why could you not train people as each machine was installed and parts of the building were being finished? In this way, they were able to find ways to run large parts of these previously assumed sequential tasks in parallel."

"Okay, I think I get you Tim. With the teams looking at revenues (throughput of the organization as you would say) as opposed to just the sub-project goals, they focused on the real value of the project. By building the schedule backward from this goal, they could really look at what items were the most important."

"Exactly."

"Hmm, I get the 'set the right goal/throughput' part. We talked about goal setting in my MBA classes. The 'building schedules back to front' part is more of a Gary thing. Perhaps you could walk through an example of this with him."

"Sure."

"Tim, goal setting and building schedules back to front does not sound like something exclusive to Critical Chain."

"Sort of. It is an important piece of building a Critical Chain schedule. And Critical Chain looks at pulling several project management best practices together and having them reinforce each other so it creates a complete solution. You can use some pieces individually and use them with other methodologies, but you would then miss out on the full and combined benefit when you use all of the techniques together."

"Sure Tim, synergy. The value of the parts working together is greater than the sum of their individual pieces."

Organizational Analysis to Better Understand the Environment (Creating the CRT and FRT)

"So Randal, this is the last major piece."

"Sounds good Tim! My head is spinning and I'm almost out of coffee."

"So Randal, when you implement any process, its success and value heavily depend on the environment you are implementing the solution into. If the culture does not support the solution, it will not work. If the process only addresses part of the organization's problems, then the new process may fail to work. This is true for Critical Chain, Agile, Scrum, and so on."

"Makes sense, Tim. It also explains why some organizations have great success with a proven solution, and others fail miserably with the exact same process. The organization's willingness to adopt the solution as well as its culture, and the nature of the organization all heavily influence the level of success. I've seen case studies highlighting this point time and time again."

"So the Theory of Constraints Thinking Process (TOC TP) provides a way to do a root cause analysis of your organizations issues. From there, you can not only see which issues the Critical Chain general solution can help you address, but, as important, you can also see what other areas you will need to work on that need to be addressed outside of the Critical Chain solution. This enables you to develop a complete and overall solution that will significantly improve your organization."

"Makes sense. Can you possibly show me an example another time?"

"Sure."

Mixing Multiple Project Management Methodologies

"So Randal, all of these areas come to come together to make a more rigorous project management system. We can use the organizational analysis to look at the company's environment and use Critical Chain to ensure the projects are planned and executed based on bottom line impact and effectively manage project variability."

"Hey Tim, what about other solutions such as extreme programming, Lean, and Agile? Are all of these mutually exclusive?"

"You can certainly mix project management methodologies, but you really need to have a solid grounding in each of the methodologies you are trying to mix. For example, I have seen people use Critical Chain for the high-level strategic schedule and use Scrum to drive the tactical deliverables into the high-level schedule. In some cases it works really well. In some cases it is put together incompletely and gets poor results. If you really want to learn more about combining methodologies like Lean, Six Sigma, and TOC, take a look at the book *Velocity*."

Wrapping Up

"So Randal, we covered several items:

- Common Issues that Critical Chain can help you address
- Common benefits of Critical Chain
- Some sample results
- Key components that enable Critical Chain to achieve its results and benefits"

"It's quite a list Tim, and much more complete and thought-out than what I heard our engineering team did. Would you be able to spend some time and

Get it Done On Time!

meet with Gary and walk through the details a bit more? He lives this project management stuff more than I do and it could end up really helping us."

Tim paused a bit, thinking about all of the work he was getting himself into. It takes a lot of effort and commitment to put a new process, any process, into place. "Hmm, are you sure Randal?"

"Definitely," Randal says, looking a bit excited, "I have talked to Gary several times during my internship. He really needs help and is a bit shy to ask for it. You have a really good handle on this solution and I think he would find it interesting. If we can get results even half as good as the examples you explained, it would really help us out. I'll set up a meeting for us."

"Sounds good, Randal. My schedule is pretty open."

"Perfect! I'll work with Gary to set up a meeting. I will also see if we can set you up with a brief consulting contract. I figured while you are helping us out, it couldn't hurt to pay you a bit for your time and effort," Randal says with a smile. "I'll e-mail you specifics shortly."

Current Reality Tree (CRT)

As their meeting wraps up, Randal heads out and Tim takes out a piece of paper and starts to jot down some of the issues he and Randal had discussed (items denoted as [crt #] above). Then Tim started drawing arrows on how they are loosely connected. After sketching it out, he started to review it. Then Tim hears...

"What is that?"

Looking up, Tim is a little surprised to see Randal. "I thought you left."

"I forgot my keys," Randal states as he waves them in front of Tim.

"I see."

"So is your diagram related to our company?"

"Actually, it is. I had mentioned that the TOC Thinking Process organizational analysis is helpful in understanding the company's environment. It takes a while to build and gather up all of the data to make it. Based on our conversation I wanted to sketch out a few of the items we discussed. I figured I could possibly show you the organizational analysis once it was done." Thinking for a moment, he continues, "Then again, if you want to see what I have so far, I'm fine with sharing it with you."

"Sure Tim. A picture is worth a thousand words. So what do you call this diagram?"

"The first page is the Current Reality Tree or CRT for short."

Chapter 2 | High-Level Critical Chain Overview

Curiously, Randal inquires, "And what is the CRT diagram used for?"

"It captures the current issues an organization is facing, how they inter-relate, and what the core drivers of those issues are. This allows me to have a quick summary of your organization, see what the key issues are, and where to focus our efforts. They can get pretty complex. This one is just a summary."

Randal pulls up a chair, "Can you walk me through it?"

"Um, sure," Tim says, feeling a bit odd. Usually he waits until someone has gotten more familiar with Critical Chain or TOC before sharing an analysis.

Randal stares at it briefly, trying to figure it out and then asks, "So is there a special way you are suppose to read it?"

"Sure," says Tim and he proceeds to review the CRT with Randal.

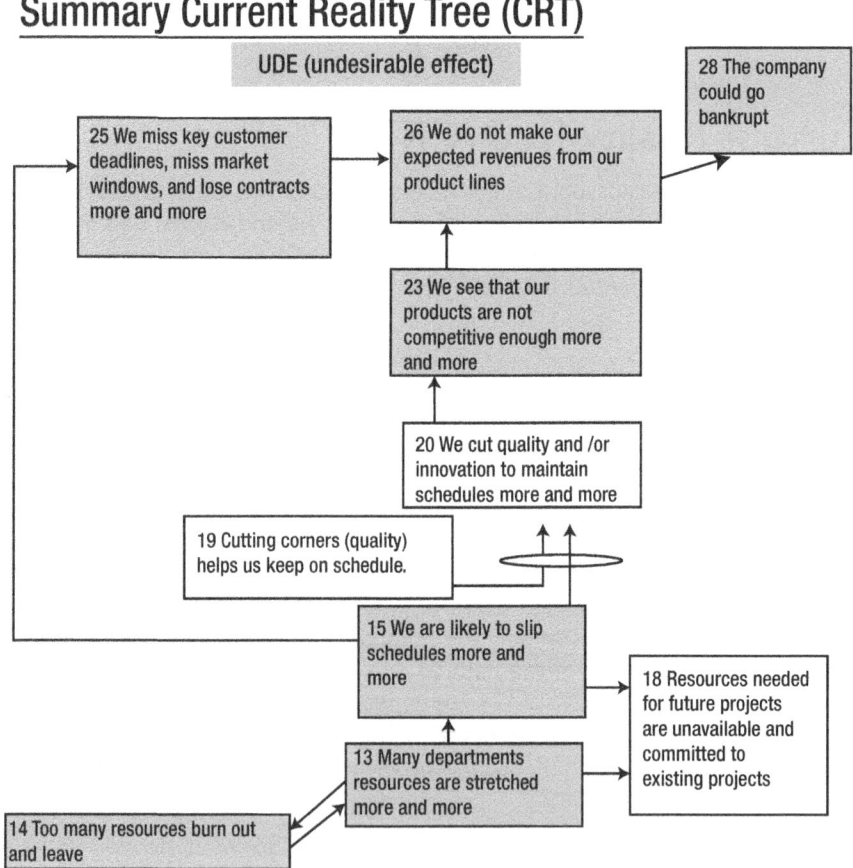

Get it Done On Time!

"So Randal, the CRT is like a logical proof based on if-then logic and dependencies. For now, I am just sketching out some of the issues and connecting them with rough logic and long arrows. From example, starting at the bottom of the chart if 14) too many resources leave the company, then one consequence is that 13) departments get stretched out."

"Makes sense, I guess. As we unfortunately lose people, it will add pressure to the department that lost that person. What about the other arrows?"

Tim continues, "The stretched out departments lead to 15) schedules slipping."

"Kinda of a jump there, Tim. If resources leave, well, sure it puts pressure on the schedules, but there are other reasons why our schedules slip."

"True. Like I said it is with long arrows, but as you noted it is insufficient by itself. There are other issues that impact schedules that we'll need to capture."

"Fair enough."

"So continuing, 13) departments being stretched and 15) the slipping schedules lead to 18) resources for future projects are being delayed."

"Makes sense. We are trying to get the current projects out so the future projects suffer."

"Yes. 15) We slip schedule then 19) and 20) cutting corners will keep us on schedule that leads us to 23) we've cut too much and we're not competitive."

"Yuck, I see that on both sides. Engineering is under pressure to make deadlines and marketing is complaining that our products are not competitive enough."

"Then 23) being not competitive leads to 26) we miss our expected revenues. And in addition to that, 15) we slip schedules leads to 25) we miss market windows and lose contracts, which also leads to 26) we miss revenues and finally that leads to 28) the company goes bankrupt."

"Not very pretty, Tim. But yes in a rough way you seem to have captured our concerns. Is there a bright side to this analysis?"

Future Reality Tree (FRT)

"Sure Randal. The Future Reality Tree is the vision of where we want to move. It includes key items we need to put into place and the benefits we want to obtain." Tim then takes out a second sheet of paper and jots down some of the desired benefits he and Randal discussed before (items denoted as [frt #] above).

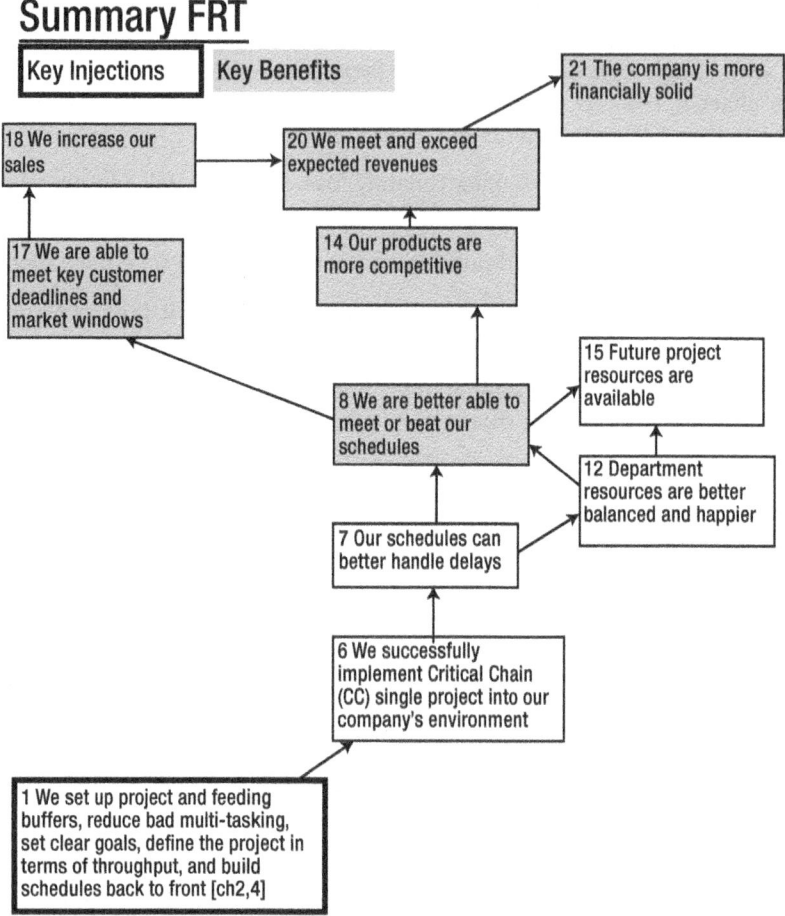

"Starting at the bottom of the chart, if we 1) set up project buffers, reduce bad-multi-tasking, set clear goals, define the project in terms of throughput, and build schedules back to front, we then will 6) successfully implement Critical Chain."

"I am guessing, Tim, that is not the only step we need to implement Critical Chain?"

"No, it is a key one though. As we go through the implementation, I will need to add others. Continuing, once 6) Critical Chain is implemented then 7) our schedules can better handle delays, which leads us to 8) we can better meet or beat deadlines."

"I like the sound of meeting or beating our schedules. But we have a lot of challenges and we have tried several things to improve our schedule performance. This looks a bit light."

"True Randal; it is just a start. We will need to add several more items to strengthen our ability to meet or beat our schedules."

"I also added if we have 7) better schedules then 12) department resources are better balanced. If we have 8) better delivery dates then 15) future resources should be more available."

"Okay."

"Building off 8) have better schedules then 14) our products can be more competitive and then 20) we can have better revenues. In addition, 8) better schedules leads us to 17) meeting key customer deadlines, 18) increased sales, 20) meeting revenues, and 21) the company being more profitable."

"It sounds like it is in the right direction, Tim. A bit thin, but promising. I am curious to see how your diagrams build out. For now, I'll set up that meeting with Gary and we can see where things go from there."

"Sure, Randal."

CHAPTER 3

Factors for Successful Implementations

Tim sits in the coffee shop, calmly waiting. After a few minutes, Randal enters followed by another man in his early 40s with thinning grey hair.

"Hi Tim, please meet Gary, our engineering manager. He's excited to hear more about your TOC expertise and he can fill in any engineering and scheduling specifics we need."

"Hello Gary, it is good to finally meet you," says Tim.

"Hi Tim," says Gary a bit cautiously, "Randal has told me you have quite a bit of experience with Critical Chain project management and he thought you would be able to help us out."

"Yes. I am looking forward to it," replies Tim.

"So Tim," Randal says a bit sheepishly, "Just to let you know, I'm closing out a few loose ends with your contract. Once that is taken care of, I can get your office and security badge set up."

"Sounds good. Thanks Randal. So Gary, Randal said that you have already started looking into Critical Chain?"

"Well Tim, we tried Critical Chain at our company and it looked promising, but it did not seem to work very well."

"Interesting. Can you let me know who helped you put the Critical Chain methodology into place?" inquires Tim.

"Actually we did some research looking at a few white papers and articles we found on the Internet," Gary dryly replies.

"So Gary I assume no one is certified in Critical Chain, the TOC Thinking Process, and has prior experience in implementing Critical Chain at your organization?"

"Well, not really. The concepts seemed pretty straightforward at the time. You know set up some buffers, tell people not to multi-task, and all that."

Tim sighs, "On a high level, the Critical Chain concepts are simple. In fact they can be deceptively simple. Yes, the ideas and concepts on the surface are pretty straightforward, but the details and what is really needed to successfully put them into place can be pretty involved."

"Tim, is this your consultant speak for saying we might of overlooked some things?" inquires Randal.

"When you are getting started with any process you can certainly read up and get some initial experience implementing it. But it also helps to have someone with prior experience to help look things over as well so you can learn from them what works and does not work."

"So Tim on that note, a quick question," asks Gary.

"Sure."

"Randal tells me you were just recently let go?"

"Yes."

"And you are trying to apply some of your TOC concepts there?"

"Yes."

"Yet the company failed, Tim?"

"I see your point, Gary. Well, I can share a few things with you. First I can point out a few other implementations I've done as well as references for them."

"That would be helpful, Tim."

"As far as my prior company, I was hired to help out with project management. Critical Chain was something the organization was not familiar with, but were initially open to hearing about. As I started working on improving their schedules, I looked at applying Critical Chain and some of its principles. The company was very rooted in their existing process. So I had to implement schedules their way, but I was working on influencing some of their key people. It takes time and the company's funding ran out before I was able to get them to try a pilot."

"I see," replies Gary. "Well, we can continue to look at Critical Chain, but I will be looking for solid reasons and justification. I'll also want to talk to some of your references. That will help me feel a bit more comfortable implementing something established."

Key Characteristics of Successful Implementers and Implementations [frt 2]

Tim looks over a bit at Randal and then at Gary. "So Gary, as we discussed we both want to be successful with implementing Critical Chain. Just be aware it is not enough to try to implement the concepts. In my experience, I've seen several things contribute to *successful implementations*:

- A Critical Chain implementation expert who really understands the mechanics of the Critical Chain solution, including how to use it correctly to help organizations increase throughput, and how to successfully implement it in an organization.
- Someone who has Critical Chain software tool experience.
- For complicated and political environments, I personally like to see someone who has a Theory of Constraints thinking process background that can do an organizational analysis.
- The organization has a compelling need and desire to change.
- We set up the correct metrics."

"Interesting list, Tim," states Gary.

"So Gary, let me walk through each of these, one-by-one."

Critical Chain Implementation Expert

First, you need a *Critical Chain implementation expert* who really understands the solution. Someone who understands the mechanics of the solution (creating buffers, removing safety at the task level, etc.). You also need someone who understands how to use the Critical Chain solution to increase the organization's throughput (managing constraints, Process of Ongoing

Improvement (POOGI), reducing bad multi-tasking, and so on). In regards to understanding Critical Chain, the question is—where and how did they learn about Critical Chain? Did they just read a book and wing it? Where were they trained? Are they *certified* and what is the background of the organization that certified them? Is it a methodology-based organization or a tool-based organization?

The second and very critical part is *experience*. How many implementations have they done? What were the results? What is their process? Have they done implementations in organizations or industries similar to yours? If the results were so good, is there someone who would be willing to be a reference that you can talk to?

"So Tim, you are saying there is a whole set of expertise involved in understanding the solution and being able to implement it into an organization?" inquires Gary.

"Exactly, expertise and experience. For example, I went through certification training on Critical Chain and the Theory of Concepts thinking process, and I went through the recommendations process at the Goldratt Institute. I am not an expert to the degree they are, but I am familiar with the mechanics of the solution and using it to move an organization to increase throughput as a whole. I've worked at implementing TOC at several companies. Some of those implementations went well, and as with my last company, some did not."

"So Tim, is this expertise and experience something we could eventually bring in house to our organization?" asks Gary.

"Yes, in fact it is necessary to help the solution succeed. I can help with training your team in the methodology. Your team in turn will then be responsible for managing and setting up future schedules using the methodology."

"Okay, Tim. I will need a better understanding from you as far as what is involved in the team training. How long will it take? What benefits we should expect?"

"Sure, Gary. Not a problem! That will be part of the implementation plan I can provide."

Critical Chain Software Tool

"So Gary, the second point is having *Critical Chain software tool experience*. To support a Critical Chain implementation, you need software that supports the Critical Chain methodology. Which Critical Chain software vendor does your Critical Chain implementer recommend and why? Who can provide training and support in the software tool to best support your organizations needs? As a customer, have you compared the pros and cons of the various Critical Chain software solutions? Without the Critical Chain software, it is difficult to impossible to effectively manage the projects within the Critical Chain methodology."

"That part I guess makes sense. We were just trying to make it work with MS Project," replies Gary.

"Gary that is a good starting point, but when it comes to actually putting the Critical Chain buffers in, identifying the Critical Chain, and managing the buffer consumption, it is a lot easier if your project management tool can support the Critical Chain methodology. I have seen a few good Critical Chain software tools, and like everything, each one has its advantages."

"I guess that makes sense. Is the Critical Chain software expensive? Is it scalable?"

"Gary, we can pilot with a few licenses. As your needs grow, you can decide if a site license makes sense."

"Sounds reasonable, Tim. We can start small, review the results, make sure it is addressing our needs, and scale up as it makes sense from there."

TOC Thinking Process Background

"So the third successful characteristic is having the *Theory of Constraints Thinking Process (TOC TP) background*. So for complicated and political environments, I really like to see someone who has a Theory of Constraints thinking process background that can do an organizational analysis. It helps get everyone on the same page regarding the project management issues everyone shares, highlight the costs of these combined issues, and the value and steps needed to switch to a new system. The organizational analysis also highlights that there may be several things that need to be addressed in addition to just implementing the Critical Chain solution. For example, if the organization lacks good requirements management, basic project management fundamentals, or has policies that make sense locally but could hinder the overall organization's success, the organizational analysis will help highlight these areas. The analysis will help us with creating an overall picture."

"Tim, I can kinda see your point here," Randal jumps in. "I have put together simple marketing processes and the changes were fairly easy to do within our own department. When it came to trying to make our entire organization customer focused, we not only had to change marketing, but get the whole organization—engineering, sales, marketing, and HR—to align and work with us. It was really challenging, time consuming, often dragged things to a halt, and caused us to put several compromises into our overall solution."

"Exactly. When you start crossing and trying to coordinate multiple departments, it can become a much larger issue. This is where the Theory of Constraints thinking process can help significantly."

Compelling Reason to Change

So the forth point is *that the organization needs to have a compelling reason to change*. Desperation works best, but a really strong drive to keep succeeding, desire to grow, or vision can work too. Companies losing key customers due to repeatedly missing deadlines or under strong competition are by nature more willing to take steps to change and improve their processes... or they will simply be driven out of business. Organizations that see themselves as successful can often be very hard to change. They are successful, their current processes got them there, so why would they want to change or mess with what is already working so well?

Using the TOC thinking processes can help us better understand the organizational issues and clarify the significant value of changing thus helping to motivate them to improve the organizations processes. One way to look at it is a desperate situation often gets people motivated to start making changes; a determined organization is more likely to keep on the path of ongoing improvements.

Randal looks at Tim directly, "Well Tim, as we have talked before, I think that is where we are and I am sure Gary will agree. We keep missing key deadlines. We know this is critical if our company is to succeed. In addition, Micky, our interim CEO, is very determined to make a difference and significantly grow the company. So he is not willing to sit idle with what has been done in the past as well."

Gary looks over at Tim with a sigh, "Actually Tim, the missing deadlines situation is getting pretty bad; engineering has been slipping features and schedules for a while [crt 15]. This in turn has stressed our customers and in some cases caused us to renegotiate existing contracts and lose some future contracts [crt 25]. This has put Micky a bit on the war path. He is working to amend agreements with our customers and find new contracts to replace the lost ones, but he is infuriated by engineering for putting him into this position. Rumor is that if we do not dramatically change things soon the company will be out of business within a year [crt 28]."

Randal looks at Gary with a bit of shock. "I did not realize things were that severe."

"We have some time Randal, but we need to make changes and do something quickly and it needs to make a significant difference," says Gary. "That is why Tim talking to you is very timely."

Tim pauses for a little bit. "Randal you said Micky was the interim CEO; can you clarify this a bit for me?"

"Sure thing, Tim. Roger was our last CEO. Great guy. Had a good feeling for the overall business. Engineering, marketing, the customers. He had a good sense of it all. Well, he ran into some medical issues. So he has temporarily stepped down so he could focus on the issues and spend some more time with his family. Micky pitched that he could cover for Roger and the board approved it."

"And one more thing, Tim," Randal says, continuing. "Micky was the Director of Marketing and is a pretty aggressive guy. He is great with customers and contracts. He sees this as his big play to move up. He wants to deliver outstanding results so the board will keep him in the CEO spot and he is hell bent on it."

"Interesting…interesting," thinks Tim. "Thank you for letting me know, Randal."

"Sure Tim, I just want to be sure you don't get bored."

Everyone pauses on that thought for a minute…

Setting Up the Correct Metrics

"So Gary, one last item. I have seen it where Critical Chain implementations have gone really well and the team is successful and then the whole thing gets unraveled by executive management. Management looks for ways to make the schedules more aggressive or pushes traditional metrics into a Critical Chain schedule. It is a bit disheartening after all of the hard work that goes in."

"Tim, I am not sure I entirely follow you. Can you give a few examples?"

"Sure, Gary. So Critical Chain works by driving teams to work on aggressive focus times and then using a project buffer to protect the overall deadline. Some managers feel that if they pile on work and drive their teams to very aggressive deadlines, they will get more out of their teams. So when these managers see the schedule with the focused time finishing weeks to months ahead of the buffered date, they want their teams to commit to delivering to the aggressive focused time or they want the teams to cut the size of the project buffer."

"I think I can see your point Tim," states Randal. "I could see Micky being that aggressive."

"The problem, Randal, is that the aggressive focus times are exactly that. If everything goes perfectly well the dates would work, but that is completely unrealistic and never happens. So the teams that are forced to meet an overly aggressive date will miss it and then management will blame the team and the Critical Chain methodology for not working."

"So Tim, what do you do in these cases?" inquires Gary.

"It depends on the level of trust. If exec management is willing to learn and work with the Critical Chain methodology, then we can openly discuss aggressive focus times and the project buffer. If exec management is not that involved then it is best to focus on the team's committed deadline (the end of the project buffer) and focus discussions on how well they are tracking to meet this deadline."

"That makes some sense Tim," states Gary. "It has always been a balance for us when we provide dates to the execs. It has to be both aggressive and realistic. Although our definitions and their definitions of what this means can vary a great deal."

"True, the metrics also require managers to change how they manage their teams."

"What do you mean, Tim?"

"If we move the teams to work with focus times, we know that sometimes they will run late. We cannot punish them. If we do they will start padding their dates more and more and that will undermine the point of having focused times."

"Hmm, that will be tricky Tim. We need accountability."

"True. In the next meeting we can talk about the rate that the project buffer gets consumed as a way to help manage the project. At this time, just note for Critical Chain the focus is on the overall project deadline and less on the individual deadlines."

"Fair enough, Tim. I can appreciate the points you make in regards to successful implementations, but I really need to see the details you have regarding the mechanics of the solution so I can understand how Critical Chain is going to deliver the results we need."

"Sure Gary; perhaps we can talk more about the Critical Chain mechanics in our next meeting."

Environmental Factors

"So Tim," Randal interjects, "By finding a wiz-bang TOC consultant like yourself to help us with the points you mention can we pretty much guarantee the success and results we need?"

"It's not that simple, Randal. If you find a wiz-bang TOC consultant, your odds of succeeding significantly increase, but there are still a variety of issues that could happen as well. Critical Chain is not just the mechanics of how you set up a schedule. Ideally you are changing and improving the process, culture, and overall way the organization approaches projects."

Randal looks a bit crestfallen. "Tim, you are starting to sound like a glass half empty kinda guy. So I see from the implementation side what you think is needed, but from our side—the client side—are there issues that could derail an implementation?"

"Randal, the possible problems can be endless, but some of the main *organizational* issues I have seen include:

- Does the organization's project team take ownership of the Critical Chain solution? If you have not won them over and they do not understand what you are trying to achieve and how, it will limit or prevent your success.

- Has senior management bought into the solution? Do you have a senior manager who is the organization's TOC champion? Does management understand what Critical Chain changes and how they need to change what they manage and focus on? If not, they may try to make changes that violate the methodology and limit your success. They also may actively or passively fight adding the new methodology that they do not understand or threatens what they were used to, even though you are trying to use the new methodology to improve the organization.

- The other way of looking at it is your department independent and isolated enough that you can set up and manage schedules how you want without senior management involvement as long as you deliver products successfully?

- How complex is your project environment? It is more straightforward to implement Critical Chain in a small simple single project environment than a large heavily matrixed multiple project environment?

- How good is the organization's project management practices? If the organization does not have basic project management fundamentals, it makes implementing a more developed project management methodology difficult. Critical Chain can help underscore key practices, but the organization will still need to have a plan to develop the project management basics as far as requirements gathering, charters, managing requirements, planning, etc. www.pmi.org is one organization that helps with overall project management certifications."

"So Tim, all these issues pretty much make Critical Chain a difficult solution to implement?"

"Overall Randal, these organizational issues are not Critical Chain specific. They are general organizational issues that could make implementing *any* project management methodology (Critical Chain, scrum, agile,) hard or impossible to successfully implement. There is a cost-benefit decision. Do you understand what is involved in putting the solution into place, what benefits you are looking for, and does the cost justify the benefits? The benefits and improved organizational throughput should be significant enough to justify the cost of putting the new solution, training, and changes in place."

"Well Tim, I guess the same is true for our company as well. The more we understand Critical Chain and the characteristics and factors you mentioned, the better we can help move the implementation along as well as make sure the person I have helping implement it in our organization is covering everything we need."

"Exactly Randal, and sometimes you might have different people cover different roles. One person might focus on the organization issues where another specializes in the Critical Chain software."

Gary looks over, "Tim, engineering is pretty swamped already. There is no way we have the time for our resources to work on making an organizational change."

"No worries Gary," Randal jumps in. "That is what Tim is for. He is to help guide and educate us;. He will help make the transition as smooth as possible and work with me on moving management."

"Okay, Randal. But we should be clear on roles and responsibilities," states Gary.

"Sure Gary," states Randal.

Wrapping Up

"So to move things forward, we should look at the following," Randal continues:

- Tim, can you work with Gary to improve the project team's understanding of Critical Chain.
- I will work with Tim on getting senior management buy-in. Micky, the interim CEO, definitely sees a need to improve project management. We just need to gather some real results first to help convince him why this approach will work.

- Tim, environment wise, I think we're okay. We have several projects running in parallel, but we're not a Fortune 500 company yet.
- Gary, what is your take on our project management practices?

"Randal," Gary says, now a bit more confident, "I think we're okay. Our project managers have good experience and know our projects. We did some initial research with Critical Chain, so we know some of the concepts. What we really need is for Tim to help us understand the concepts in more detail and help us get better results without thrashing the projects we are working on currently." Turning to Tim, he says, "Tim, can we walk through the concepts in a lot more detail in our next meeting? I really need to see how they are going to work so I can feel confident that they will actually help us get back on track."

"Sure Gary. I will set up a meeting for it."

Randal looks around, "Any other issues?" Randal sees that no one speaks up. "Good then, sounds like we have the starting of a plan."

Future Reality Tree (FRT)

As Gary heads out, Tim waits a few minutes and takes out the piece of paper he has been drawing the Future Reality Tree (FRT) on.

Randal lingers behind and looks on, "More boxes to add to your chart?"

"Just one," says Tim.

Chapter 3 | Factors for Successful Implementations

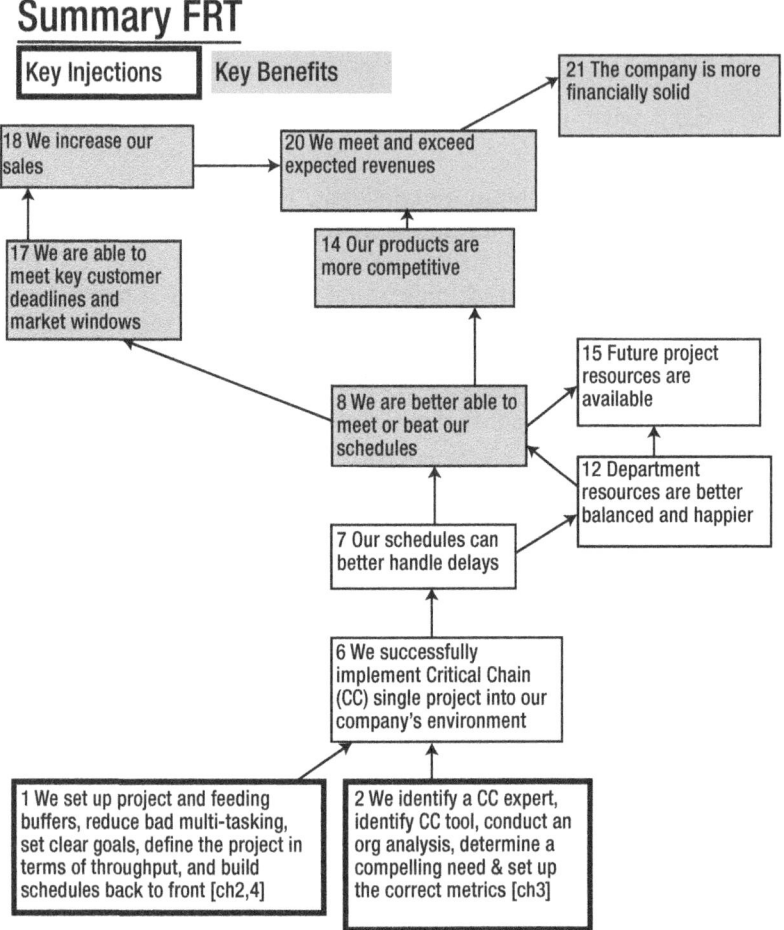

Tim says to Randal, "In order to 6) successfully implement Critical Chain what is needed? We need 1) to understand and implement the Critical Chain concepts. We also 2) need to be aware of the factors for successful implementations. A good start, but there are still a few more items needed to help us successfully implement Critical Chain."

"I see, Tim. Your tree is pretty thin. Is the goal to fill the page with boxes?"

"Not really. I'm just trying to capture the key items that are needed. As we get further along, the page will fill up."

CHAPTER 4

How Does the Critical Chain Solution Work?

Tim sits in the coffee shop idly waiting for Randal and Gary, again. Then he sees something so bright, so shocking, so… pink. "Randal, your pink shirt is hurting my eyes."

"Tim, it's not pink, it's salmon. And being a marketing guy, we like to stand out."

"Well, you certainly have succeeded. Any luck with the office setup?"

"I was able to find you an office; now it's just a matter of getting a phone and computer."

"I see. Hi Gary, how are you?"

"I am doing well Tim; sorry to hear about the office delays. For some reason, these things take some time to get setup. But at least we can meet at the coffee shop. Things have been getting pretty tense, so it is good to get away for a few minutes."

"So Tim, what did you want to cover today?" says Randal.

© Eric Bergland 2016
E. Bergland, *Get it Done On Time!*, DOI 10.1007/978-1-4842-1860-0_4

Chapter 4 | How Does the Critical Chain Solution Work?

"Well, as Gary noted last time, I think it's important we dive a bit deeper into how Critical Chain works so we can be sure we understand the different concepts."

"Sounds technical," says Randal cautiously.

"We need the details. Think about it like peeling an onion. We need to understand the high-level basic concepts to start. Then we need to dig into the concepts a bit deeper on the implementation level, which is this conversation. We will then need to go through the implementation steps and plan on how we will put Critical Chain into place, which we can cover next time."

"Tim, how do the different managers, project managers, and engineers learn about the concepts?" asks Gary.

"That is a good question. As part of the implementation plan, we set up different training courses focused on the needs of the individuals. The managers need to understand the concepts on a strategic level. The software engineers need a basic overview so they understand how the solution impacts them and what they need to do to support it. The project managers need training on the concepts and how to manage the project under Critical Chain."

"Well, try to keep it fun Tim. I don't want you to put me to sleep."

"I'll try Randal, but we need to go a bit deeper on the key concepts. The training course will also go into more detail. But it is important for you and Gary to really understand the concepts if you are going to help implement them."

"Fair enough, Tim."

Key Critical Chain Benefits

"There are a variety of books, white papers, and classes that overview Critical Chain concepts. But to summarize, I would say the *key Critical Chain benefits* [frt 1] that help us get results are:

- Project and feeding buffers are used to manage variability
- Reducing bad multi-tasking to find hidden or misused resource capacity
- Defining the project goal and building schedules back-to-front
- Organizational analysis (TOC Thinking Process) to better understand the company's work environment and issues that could impact the success of our implementation

"Okay Tim, some of those I have heard about with our past research and implementation," states Gary.

"Good, having some familiarity helps us out. So Gary let's walk through them one by one in more detail just to be sure we have it covered. Let me know if you have any questions. We will try not to lose Randal," Tim says with a smile.

"Hey, I heard that," Randal says, looking up from his coffee cup.

Project and Feeding Buffers
Padding Dates:

"So let's start with *buffers*. You have already seen why you need buffers [Chapter 2], but now let's look at how Critical Chain sets them up. I will assume you are familiar with the management practice of *padding due dates*, Randal?"

"In the sense that I know engineers often miss their commitment dates, so I ask them to deliver to an earlier date, knowing it is very likely they will miss it. Then it is a guessing game of what date I really think they will really hit."

"Well Randal, on a simple level that works; on more complex projects it gets tricky. For a yearlong project, how much can you pad the due dates without someone else calling it out and cutting it? With tight deadlines, will the schedule even allow you to add additional time to protect the deadline sufficiently? Do you have a formal way to manage this padding? What happens to your schedule when the engineers know there is really more time than you are saying?"

"Okay, okay, Tim. The padding works well on a task level, but on a large project it does not work as well. But Tim, everyone does it. The engineers pad their task estimates and management pads the overall project estimates. The irony is that the projects still come in late and the padding can make the project length so huge and unrealistic we end up cutting time estimates like crazy. *It is a big poker game.* How much time can the engineers get management to add to the schedule to ensure features and quality versus how much time managers can cut from the engineers' estimates to manage costs and hit key market windows? Unfortunately, neither way is without its consequences."

Project Buffers:

"Well Randal, that's where Critical Chain comes in. The focus is on the *strategic* use of that padding or safety time. We want to pull the safety time out of each of the tasks where it can get wasted, and we want to aggregate and move that safety time to the end of the project. In Critical Chain terms, we create a *project buffer*. In this way the safety time of the project better protects the overall project's deadline, which is critical, as opposed to using the safety time to somewhat protect each task's deadline and offer limited protection to the overall project deadline."

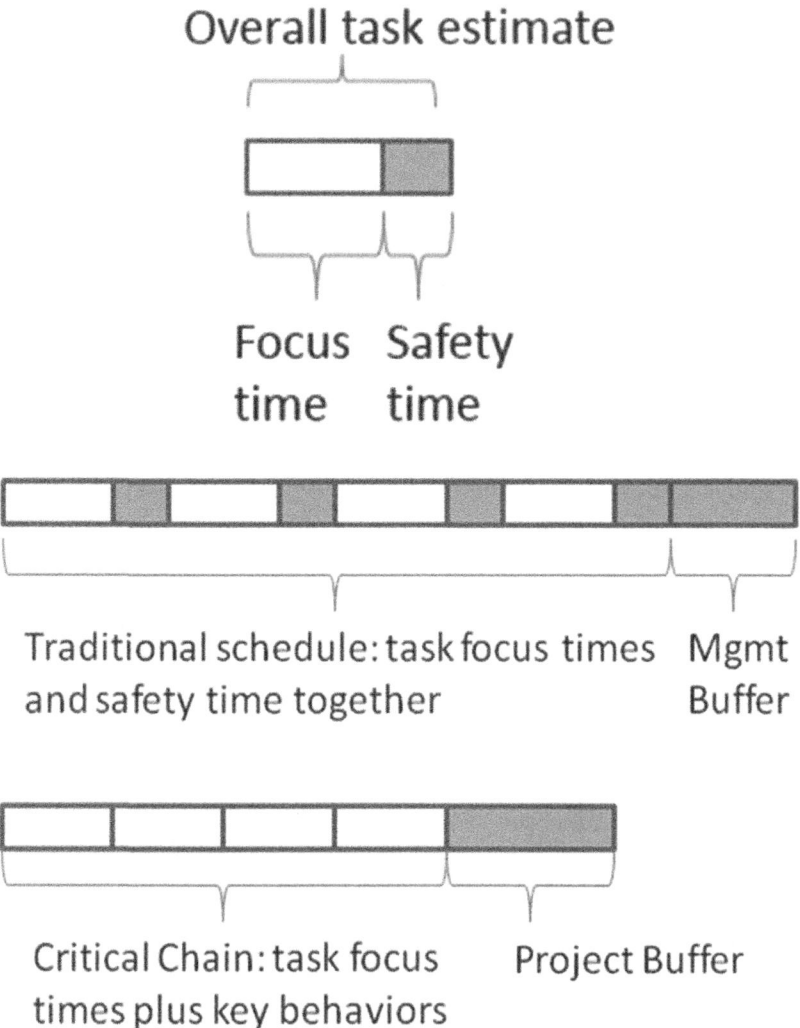

"So Tim," asks Gary, "I understand the idea of putting a buffer at the end of the project. After all, the thing I care most about is hitting our project's deadline. So how is this project buffer any different than the padding I've done in the past?"

"Well Gary, there are a few key differences. One, I am not just adding more time to the project, and lengthening it. I can actually shorten the overall project duration by being more strategic with the time I have. This is done in two ways. By removing safety from the tasks, I am pulling time out of the schedule. By putting the safety at the end of the project, I get the most value out of this time. By implementing some key behaviors such as roadrunners, relay races, reducing bad multi-tasking, and trying to eliminate student syndrome, I waste less time. Between the strategic buffer and behaviors I can reduce the overall schedule duration compared to a traditional schedule."

"Wow Tim, you just threw out a bunch of new terms; can you clarify them?"

"Sure Gary. I can walk through them more in the Critical Chain training, but on a high level, *roadrunner* refers to the fact that we want resources to start working on a task as soon as the project manager sees that the task is ready to be worked on and has assigned it to the resource. *Relay race* is that as soon as a task is finished, we want to execute a clean, quality hand-off to the next resource so they can start right away. *Bad multi-tasking* is when resources work inefficiently on several tasks at once. *Student syndrome* is the temptation to put work off to the last minute. This can also be paired with bad multi-tasking in the sense that I will not start a task right away, but I will work on one task and then only switch over when I realize the deadline is coming up for another task. All these behaviors impact the amount of time it takes to complete our schedule."

"I'll need a bit more of a walkthrough, but on a high level I think I see what you are saying," states Gary. "Basically there are a variety of ways people act during a project and these can have an impact on how long it takes the project to complete. So with the right behaviors in place, the project might be able to finish faster."

"Correct Gary. The second part to why project buffers are different than just padding is that I can compare the rate that I consume the project buffer to the progress I am making in completing the project. If I am using up the time in my project buffer quickly, but not making much progress in my project, I know there is a problem. I can project out this trend [fever chart] and see if my project is still meeting or likely to miss my deadline way before I actually miss it and I can start to put response plans into place to recover before I am actually late. Once traditional schedules start to fall really behind there is no *inherent* mechanism to recover. You just have to replan when it becomes too late to recover."

"Interesting, Tim. We certainly need a better way to manage delays. Will the training cover some examples so we can get some experience to better understand how this works?"

"Definitely Gary, I will be sure to include some exercises in the team training."

Feeding Buffers:

"So the project buffers protect our end date. To help protect the project buffer, we create *feeding buffers*." [frt 1]

"You kinda lost me there, Tim. What is a feeding buffer?"

"Okay Randal, pretend we are making a car. In a simple world, the engine gets built, the transmission gets built, and the car body is built. We then need to assemble them to make the car."

"Simple enough."

"If any one of these are late, we're stuck. For example, if the car engine is a week late, we have to wait a week to finish the car. If the transmission is a few days late, we have to wait a few days. We need all three components to be available at the same time."

"Again, that makes sense," says Randal.

"Tim, isn't this the nature of the project? There are often multiple paths with the critical path or as you would say, the Critical Chain, being the primary one?" asks Gary.

"You are correct, Gary. Projects can often have multiple paths. But people do not always see the added risk these multiple paths add. For example, if each component had a 90% chance of arriving on time and we needed all three at the same time then we have a 90% * 90% * 90% = 73% chance that they all would be available when we need them."

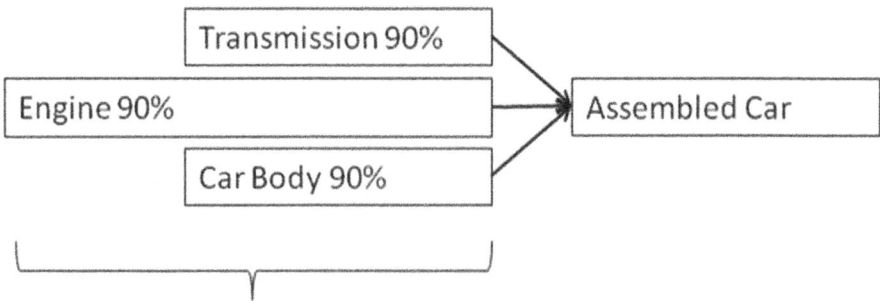

Odds all 3 are done on time 73%

"Well, that is lousy Tim," Randal says, jumping in. "27% of the time we miss our deadline. That is not acceptable."

"Exactly. So let's say the engine takes the longest to build, so it could be our Critical Chain. We will watch and monitor its progress like crazy. For the transmission and car body, they do not take as long to build, so we want to try and have them finish slightly earlier. There is a way to calculate how much feeding buffer we need, but let's say three weeks in this case. If for some reason either the transmission or car body is a few days late, then the time in the feeding buffer will absorb this delay. So instead of having a 73% combined chance of being on time we are back to 90% on time—the confidence we have that the engine will be done on time."

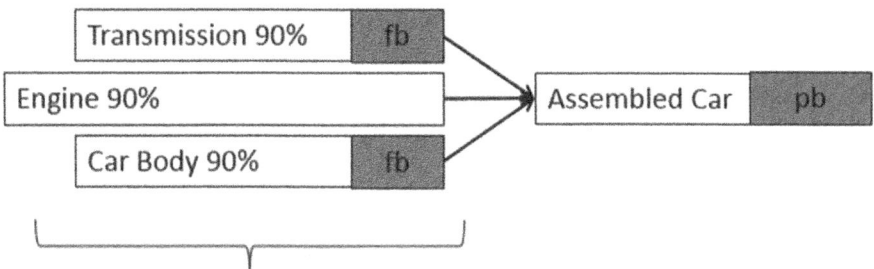

Odds all 3 are done on time 90% (assuming feeding buffers (fb) are not completely consumed).

"Okay, I think I understand Tim. The feeding buffer increases our ability to deliver on time by minimizing the number of paths that could delay our project."

"Correct, Gary. In this case, the *feeding buffers* protect the assembled car from being delayed by the transmission or car body, and the *engine* is our Critical Chain."

"I definitely like this idea Tim, and I can see where we could apply it in some of our projects to help minimize delays. I also see another point. On some past projects, we saw the critical path jump from one set of tasks to another. It really threw us off. In using the feeding buffers, I can see how it can help us. By adding some protection to the feeding paths, we both minimize their delays impacting the Critical Chain or causing them to become the Critical Chain. But one key question: where does the time for the feeding and project buffers come from, Tim?"

"Well Gary, like with the project buffer, we aggregate the safety from the tasks to strategically create the feeding buffers. The training course will cover some examples of this."

Safety Time

"So Tim, for both the project buffer and feeding buffer, you keep talking about this safety time or engineering padding. When I talk with the engineers, their schedules are pretty tight and I can't see much safety time being there if they are always late and missing their deadlines," states Randal.

Tim looks at Gary who shrugs with a smile. "That is a good point, Randal. First, let's first talk about estimates. So if you were to drive from San Francisco, CA to San Jose, CA how long would it take you?"

"About an hour, give or take."

"So Randal if you had a critical, once-in-a-lifetime interview at 5 PM for a fantastic job position, when would you leave for it?"

"Probably around 2 PM. Give myself an hour to get there, an hour buffer in case there are traffic issues, and an additional hour just in case and time to prep."

"So you have just tripled your time estimate. You said it take about 60 minutes, but you gave yourself three hours. So basically for a 60-minute task, you added two hours of safety."

"Well Tim, that is for a unique case. Not for a task estimate."

"What happens to engineers who regularly miss their deadlines, Randal?"

"Regularly? They get yelled at and possibly written up."

"And if these tasks are on the critical path?"

"Then they get really yelled at by several people, and told to shape up or they'll lose their job."

"So Randal, if you were an engineer getting yelled at all the time for missing your estimates, what type of estimates would you provide: the one hour or three hour kind?"

"I guess the three-hour estimate. I would have to start inflating my estimates, more and more, until I was confident there was no way I could miss them and people would stop yelling. Actually, if I start finishing them earlier, I would look like a hero."

"And Gary, what happens if an engineer keeps completing tasks earlier and earlier than their estimates?"

"That engineer would be accused of padding their estimates way too much and managers would start cutting their durations."

"Exactly. So the project environment encourages people to try and pad their estimates the best they can, and at the same time discourages resources from letting you know that they finished early."

"Okay, Tim I can see your point that people will try and pad their estimates. But if they have all this extra time added to the tasks, why are they still late?"

"Randal, this ties back to some of the behaviors we talked about before that can cause time to get wasted: student syndrome, Parkinson's law, bad multitasking, and so on. Overall, we just want to put the best project behaviors in place to help finish on time, report early finishes, and enable us to move the safety time from the tasks to the end of the project where the overall project gets the most benefit from it. One of the key steps in doing this is the Critical Chain training we do for the resources and project managers."

"Tim what is Parkinson's law? It sounds official."

"Sure Randal, Parkinson's law in this case is simply the fact that work will fill the available time. So the more time I give a resource to do something, the more likely the resource will use all of that time. That is one of the reasons we want resources to work toward focused times as opposed to padded or buffered times."

"Is this also covered in the training?" inquires Gary. "You are covering the concepts in much more detail and in a much more applicable way than I have seen from the white papers we read."

"Yes Gary, we can cover it in the training as well. As part of the training we set up several exercises to help reinforce and see how the various concepts work together."

Overall Benefit, Managing Project Variability

"So Randal, you still look a bit perplexed."

"Well Tim, there are a good number of buffers and some overhead associated with them. Isn't there a less complicated way?"

"So Randal, here is another way to look at it. There is an endless list of what can cause a project to be late: resources that are late, tasks that take longer than expected, unexpected problems or complications, minor delays, major delays, etc."

"Makes sense."

"So if we had a magic wand and could make all the things that could cause delays go away, how hard would it be to manage a project?"

"Well Tim, other than just setting up a schedule, I guess, not very. Since there were no delays, in theory the project would just finish on time with no problems. In fact, managing a project would be trivial. But Tim, it is totally unrealistic. There are always delays, problems, and variability in project management."

"And that is a key focus of Critical Chain. Instead of ignoring or hoping delays do not happen, we try and set up ways to *manage the variability of a project* so we are less impacted by delays. The feeding buffers minimize delays from feeding paths. Moving safety time out of the tasks and into a project buffer allows us to better protect the project's overall deadline from delays, without adding additional time. The project behaviors are to help us move as quickly as we can. All of these together help make Critical Chain a more complete project management solution."

"That is interesting, Tim. Not only are the different pieces helpful, they are actually very complementary and work together to build on each other to create a more complete solution."

"Exactly, Gary."

"So Tim, how do we put these buffers into place?"

"The Critical Chain enabled software handles it for you. For example, both ProChain and Realization build on top of MS Project. You just need to enter the focused durations (times without buffers) and buffered times. The software will automatically calculate and create the project and feeding buffers in your schedule."

"So we could start using Critical Chain software in a few of our key projects fairly quickly?"

"Yes, once the team knows the Critical Chain concepts, they can use the software to help better manage their projects."

Reducing Bad Multi-Tasking

"So Randal, the next part is multi-tasking."

"Of course it is an important skill," states Randal. "In fact, we should hire people on their ability to be good multi-taskers."

"But one prone to problems too," states Tim.

Highway Analogy

"So Randal, here is one informal example. Say you are driving your fancy BMW convertible at top speed from San Francisco, CA to San Jose, CA on highway 280 at 3 AM in the morning. How long does it take you?"

"Cool! Without police, I could go at 120 miles per hour; probably half an hour," Randal states with a big grin. "Okay, more realistically we're talking 65 miles per hour, deal with a bunch of lights, and I'll be there in about an hour."

"And if it was 5:15 PM in the thick of rush hour?"

"Ouch, torture! Probably two hours and likely I'm never leaving first gear. My poor car."

"So why the difference between 30 to 60 minutes and 120 minutes? It is not like you are going any further distance wise. The work is exactly the same."

"Tim, it's rush hour! It's like sitting in a parking lot crawling inch by inch."

"So Randal, relating back to the project management example. How fast can I finish a project if it is the only thing I am focusing on and I start right away (i.e., roadrunner)?"

"Tim, probably pretty fast."

"Like driving at 3 AM with no traffic on the highway. How long will it take me to finish the same project if I am juggling and switching back and forth between several tasks at the same time and I cannot start on it right away."

"Painfully longer."

"Exactly, like driving in traffic at rush hour. The amount of work on the one specific task does not change, but juggling between all the other tasks, starting and stopping work on one task, then another task, then another task, then coming back to the original task, then switching again. It's just stretching out how long it takes to complete something."

"So Tim, you are basically saying if we flood people with work, it is like adding more cars to the highway. It works to a point, but once I go too far, I just flood the resource and all the work just slows down almost to the point of a crawl. Project rush hour."

"Exactly, Randal. Exactly. It can vary by environments, but as organizations try to put more and more simultaneous work on resources, the more likely they are at risk of really stretching out the deadlines."

"Ahh, but wouldn't the converse be true? If I reduce the overloaded resources to some reasonable level, then I would be able to speed things up."

"Very true!"

"But Tim," states Gary, "Management expects engineering to manage multiple tasks and projects simultaneously. They see this as having the workers be efficient."

"And Gary, this is the challenge. For some, having resources multi-task on several tasks or projects is seen as squeezing more work out of the resources. And if the work comes in bits and pieces, this may work. But if we are seeing the additional work stretching out timelines more and more, this is a sign of bad multi-tasking. For example, in some organizations, before Critical Chain, we can see that the resources are overloaded and switching between tasks constantly (bad multi-tasking) and it takes forever for things to finish. By adding Critical Chain, and better prioritizing and balancing the work, we take better advantage of that resource's true capacity and now we can finish projects sooner."

Bad Multi-Tasking Example

"Tim you make it sound like all multi-tasking is bad. This cannot be true, and in our environment we need to split resources across several tasks and projects. Do you have a more specific example?"

"Sure Gary. Let's say I have John the engineer working on three tasks. Each task is two weeks long and all three are assigned at the same time. John is a really hard worker and tries to get things done as soon as he can. So he spends the first week on task A and completes the work for it. But alas, the manager for task B comes by and is upset that nothing has been accomplished on his task. So John works on that for a week. Then the manager for task C comes by. What happened to my task? So John works on that task."

Task	week1	week2	week3
Task A	Xxxxx		
Task B		Xxxxx	
Task C			xxxxx

"Makes sense Tim. The different managers try to get John to finish the work for their tasks and we often have resources shared across projects or having multiple tasks they work on within the same project. So, in some manner I can see this happening."

"True Gary, but let's look at the next set of work. After task C, the task A manager comes by and it's been three weeks! John scrambles and finishes it in week 4. Then the manager for task B comes by and it's been five weeks? So John finishes that task. Then finally the manager for task C comes by and it's been six weeks! So John finishes that task under duress. So Randal, what do you see from this example?"

Project	Week 1	Week 2	Week 3	Week 4	Week 5	Week 6
Project A	xxxxx		Xxxxx			
Project B		Xxxxx		xxxxx		
Project C			xxxxx		Xxxxx	

"I certainly don't want to be John is the first thing that comes to mind."

Get it Done On Time!

"True, it is a stressful situation for John. Gary, note for a simple two-week task how long did the project managers have to wait for him to finish? Two weeks? Three weeks? Four weeks?"

"Well Tim, looking at what you wrote, it took… four to six weeks for John to finish each of the two-week tasks."

"Tim, this is crazy. Basically John is doubling and tripling the length of work for a two-week task."

"Correct, Randal. This is what we call bad multi-tasking. John did work hard and we did not even look at any lost time due to switching between projects, but overall his lead times were horrible. By doing a little of each project at a time, he ended up stretching out the duration of all three projects. So let me give another version of the same story."

"Okay."

"John is assigned the three tasks. But in working with an overall program manager, he is able to focus and have the program manager prioritize the three tasks. Task A is to be done first, then Task B, and finally task C. The only time he can switch from one project to another is if he is either blocked or he has finished that project."

"Okay, Tim."

"The first week John works on Project A. Everything seems fine, so he then spends the second week and finishes Project A. Project B and C project managers do not rush him to start their projects, but they do watch his progress on Project A so once he is done, they know he can start on the next prioritized project. So Gary, how long was the lead time for task A?"

Task	Week 1	Week 2
Task A	Xxxxx	Xxxxx
Task B		
Task C		

"Two weeks."

"And Gary, how does that compare to the previous example?"

"It is two weeks versus four weeks. Much better! He finished it twice as fast. But Tim he has not made any progress on the other two tasks and this is an ideal case."

Chapter 4 | How Does the Critical Chain Solution Work?

"True, so let's look at the next two tasks. John's now done with task A and moves onto task B. He works one week (week 3), but alas, gets blocked. He needs someone else to finish their work first, before he can do anything else. So based on our rules John starts work on task C. He works a week and then finds out that the work that was blocking him on task B is now finished. John finished task B in week 5 and then finishes task C in week 6."

Project	Week 1	week2	Week 3	Week 4	Week 5	Week 6
Project A xxxxx	Xxxxx					
Project B		xxxxx		xxxxx		
Project C			Xxxxx		xxxxx	

"So Gary, what is different for task B and C compared to the prior example?"

"Time-wise, nothing. They both finished in weeks 5 and 6 like they did last time."

"True, but what about the lead time? From when we were expected to start to when we were expected to finish, what is the difference?"

"Hmm. In the first example they were two-week tasks so I would figure week 2 or 3 John would have been done, but it ended up being week 5 and week 6, so about three weeks later. In the second example I knew he had to do task A first. So I knew it would be later."

"Tim this sounds like a much more organized way to run projects—if we can make it work correctly."

"Exactly, Randal. As you saw, we did not change the duration of the projects, but by prioritizing and by setting clear rules, each manager understood the lead times and could manage their projects and expectations accordingly. There were no major delays versus their expectations."

"But Tim, is this a realistic issue?"

"Yes, Gary. In several ways. One, if we assign multiple tasks to a resource, with unclear or conflicting priorities, we can run into the above inefficient behavior. If some of these tasks gate other tasks then we could have problems and risk stretching out our timelines unexpectedly."

"How does this tie back to the overall Critical Chain solution?" inquires Gary.

"If we allow Critical Chain resources to jump back and forth, working on different tasks or projects incorrectly, they will stretch out the project, just like the first example with the three tasks. Resources need to focus solely on finishing a task unless they become blocked."

"Would the Critical Chain software help us with this planning?"

"The software will resolve resource contentions so that a resource will not have multiple tasks assigned at the same time. But we also need to be sure that managers are not asking resources to work on multiple tasks at once and to try and minimize the resources from doing this as well."

"So, you will have to cover this in the team training."

"Correct. Gary, do you see examples of bad multi-tasking in your current project management environment? For example, resources jumping back and forth and not finishing tasks?"

"Hmm, Tim I am going to have to think about this one a bit. We certainly juggle some key resources between multiple tasks and projects. We also run into issues where there is the current project they are working, and at the same time, high-priority bug fixes for a prior release comes up. In some cases, we certainly have them jumping around trying to maximize what they are working on, in some ways we have them start multiple things at once. But as you noted, maybe we need to rethink our strategy, prioritize tasks better, have people actually finish the tasks they start, and limit the number of tasks they are trying to do at once."

"That sounds very good, Gary. In some environments it can make a big difference." Tim also thinks to himself that Gary will need to be sure to reduce bad multi-tasking as part of their single project work, but if it is a significant issue and multiple projects are impacting shared resources, Tim might have to look into the Critical Chain multi-project solution as well.

Defining the Project Goal and Building Schedules Back-to-Front

Tim continues. "So the third way we can benefit from Critical Chain is building schedules back-to-front. There are two parts to this. The first is setting a clear goal. For it to be a clear goal it needs to be measurable with a specific timeline. For example, saying we need to buy a new house is not as clear as saying that need to buy a new house under $450,000 and finish moving in before the end of the year. It needs three bedrooms. And note, one of the children is in a wheelchair. The latter is clearer and gives you much more guidance."

"Makes sense Tim, the clearer the goal the better we can identify requirements and prioritize," states Gary. "We regularly do this, but it is good to be sure we stay on top of it."

Chapter 4 | How Does the Critical Chain Solution Work?

"Good. The second part is to build schedules back-to-front. So Randal what are some of the main items that come to mind when buying and moving into a house?"

"Hmm, get a loan, find a realtor, find and buy the new house, and move everything to the new house all come to mind."

"That is a good starting point. Note one concern with just having a list of items is that we can unintentionally forget something. There is no sense of dependencies or checks with a simple list. So Randal, let me sketch out what we have already and then we can start working backward by checking dependencies."

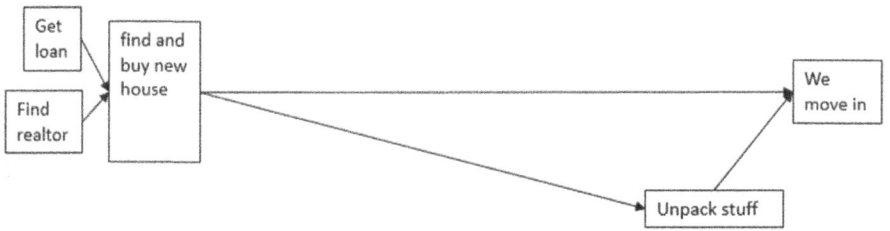

"So Randal, one of the ways we check dependencies is to use the phase in order to and we must. For example, *in order to* unpack what *must* happen immediately before it?"

"Okay, I see where you are going with this, Tim. *In order to* unpack *we must* have packed things from the old house first."

"Exactly. And when we move into our dark house with no running water or working phones we must…??"

"Run away in fearing of being in a horror movie. Just kidding, Tim. We can set up the phone, utilities, and even add Internet. And… we should probably change our address to get our mail."

"Good. So now our updated schedule looks like this…"

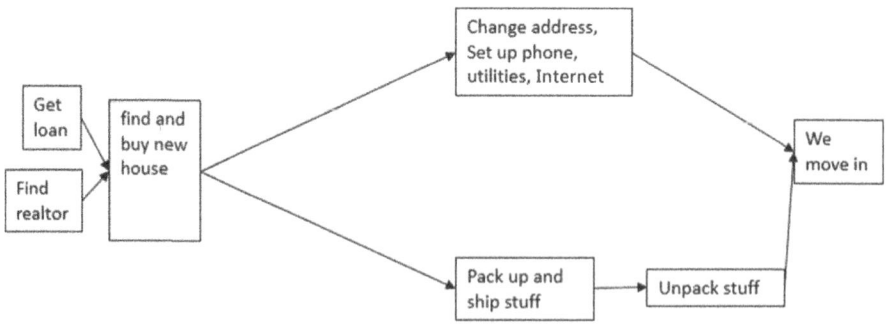

Get it Done On Time!

"So Gary, going back and checking against our goal, *in order to* buying a new house under $450,000, finish moving in before the end of the year, and one of their children is in a wheel chair *what must happen?* Did we overlook anything?"

"Hmm, Tim. We have buying the house, but it would probably be good to add the clarification that it needs to be less than $450k and purchased before the end of the year."

"True. Anything else come to mind?"

"Umm, I do not see anything about the child in the wheelchair. It would be difficult to find a wheelchair accessible house already, so more likely we would need to find a contractor, spec out changes, and remodel the existing house."

"Exactly. With the contractor and adding additional clarification, we can review and make sure we are addressing the goal of our project. So with a few more changes…"

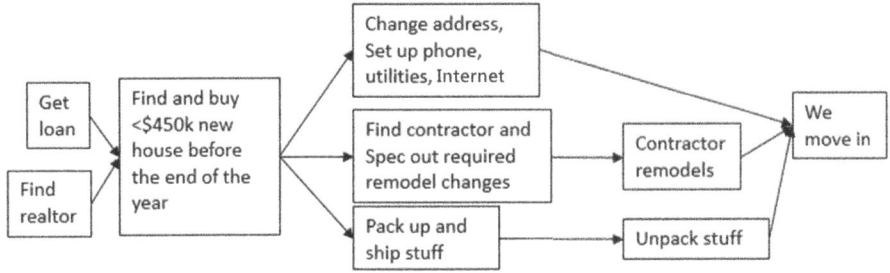

"Overall it looks okay, Tim and not to nit-pick your example, but I am sure we have missed a few things."

"True, Gary. So we can always build a schedule and then find an area expert to help us review it. For example, we did not talk about the house-purchasing process in our schedule, but if we talked with a realtor he could help us add the missing steps. The other part with Critical Chain is throughput. We want the project to have bottom line impact on the organization."

"Tim last time we talked about Harris and you had said the throughput was building the schedule out until they reached revenue," Randal recalls. "I do not see how that would work here. The family is not planning on renting out the house; they want to move in."

"Good point, Randal. Throughput is the value to the organization. For companies we can often focus on scoping the project out to the point they generate revenue. For non-profits (or the family in this case), it is more of the goal of the organization. Sure the family wants to move, but overall what are they trying to do?"

"If it was me, I would want to get settled into the new community. So sell the old house, find schools for the kids, possibly find new activities and social groups in the area."

"Exactly. I'll add in the new items you identified…"

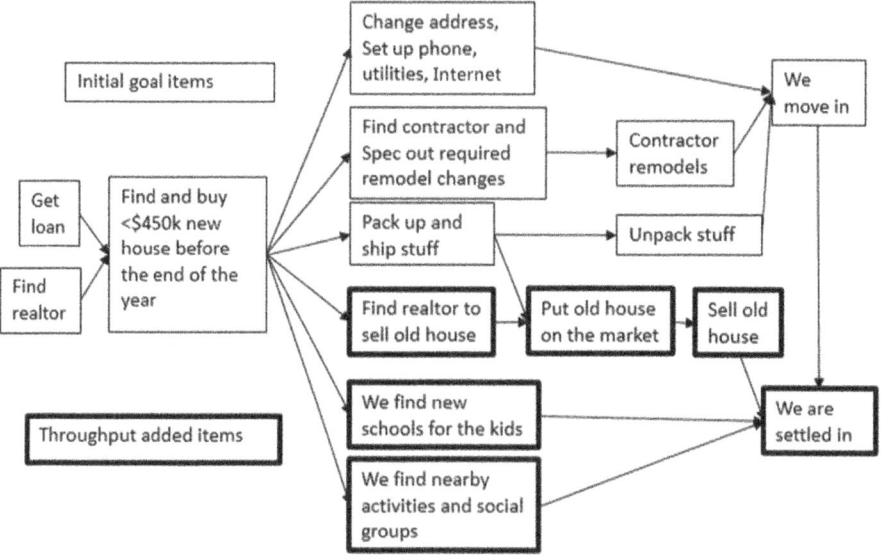

"But Tim, didn't you just complicate and make the schedule a lot more work?" inquires Randal.

"Actually Randal," Gary says, stepping in. "I think I see Tim's point. We set a goal, make sure the goal is throughput focused, and build the schedule back-to-front using *In order to* and *we must* to check dependencies. This is all part of making sure we go through and capture all of the possible work when we build out the schedule. From there, we can properly size and scope the project before it even starts and potentially minimize the number of surprises from items we might have overlooked."

"Exactly, Gary. Just a few final notes. Once the project network is constructed from back-to-front, we make a forward pass reading it from front-to-back in order to sanity check one last time for any missing dependencies or tasks. When we go from front-to-back, we read it as *if I have everything at for the first task, then is there anything else that is needed before I can work on the next task.*"

Get it Done On Time!

"You go through the network again, Tim?" asks Randal.

"Of course. The network is on paper now. It is the best time to review and challenge it. Once we begin executing the schedule, things get a lot more complicated. Actually Randal, we are still not done with the network building."

"Really?"

"Two more items. We use the *in order to.. we must* to help challenge assumptions to find missing tasks, but we also try and run as many tasks in *parallel* as we can. For example, do we have to buy the new house *before* we find a realtor to sell the old house? Same as with the Harris example."

"Harris?" inquires Gary.

"It is an example I explained to Randal where Critical Chain challenged established assumptions. By challenging assumptions they were able to find ways to run more items in parallel and compress the schedule more than people had previously thought was possible."

"Sounds interesting. We have several existing schedules already in process. Possibly you could help us review these schedules and look for opportunities."

"Sure Gary, next time we chat we could discuss it. Actually, it would be a good time for us to review the Critical Chain implementation steps."

"Tim, you had said there was one, just one, other item for building schedules??"

"Almost there, Randal. The last item is that we like to build Critical Chain schedules based on resource hand-offs. So anytime work is handed off from one resource to another, we generally like to capture it as a separate item. For example, we did not detail all of the work the contractor is doing for the remodel, but we do want to be sure we capture the hand-off of our specs to the contractor."

"Tim, can you clarify this a bit more," inquires Gary.

"Sure. Disconnects can happen between resources, so we want to be sure to capture the hand-offs."

"Makes sense, resource hand-offs are critical and can often be misaligned. But what if a particular task is huge? Like the contractor has to modify the stairways, bedrooms, floor plans, and so on. That is a lot of work to hide behind one task."

"It would be a confidence-level question Gary. If we are confident, we could have just one task for the contractor work. If it was really involved and we wanted to capture the work in more detail, we could potentially set up a separate sub-schedule detailing all the work for that task."

"Okay, Tim. Makes sense. As we work on our schedules, I will want to see how you build this out and how it works," states Gary.

Chapter 4 | How Does the Critical Chain Solution Work?

"Tim, I think I'm going to need a schedule to see how you build schedules. You have quite a few steps there," Randal says jokingly.

Organizational Analysis

"Hey Tim," Randal says, yawning a bit, "I'm kinda wearing out and I think our waitress is waiting for us to vacate the table; are we done yet?"

"Almost. The last part is organizational analysis. Often organizations look at a department's top issues or maybe even have an overall top issues list between departments. The problem is that these top issues do not highlight the interconnection between issues or root causes for the various issues. The organizational analysis, otherwise known as the TOC Thinking Process, allows us to look at the various issues the organization experiences across departments, see how they interconnect, and identify the core drivers that are causing the various problems. From there, we can see which of these problems Critical Chain can help with and which ones, outside of the Critical Chain solution, we need to address to help the overall organization improve."

"So Critical Chain does not solve every problem?"

"No Randal, there are no cure-alls. Critical Chain helps address the common project-management issues. The organizational analysis helps us identify organizational issues that could significantly limit the results of our Critical Chain implementation as well as help us see what is needed to help improve the organization as a whole. Together we get a more complete solution."

"I understand what you are saying Tim, but I dread to say I don't think we have the time to have you walk me through an organizational analysis example to better understand."

"No problem, Randal. We can cover it in more detail another time."

"Sounds good Tim," states Gary, "I like your ideas and we need to work with you on putting them into place. Micky is putting more and more pressure on engineering to make sure we are getting our projects done on time. With Critical Chain, we can work on addressing his concerns."

"Sure Gary, the next thing we need to do is to set up some training time with your team to review the concepts and begin to implement them into Critical Chain schedules. We should also set up some time so I can walk you through the implementation steps so we are sure we cover all the necessary steps for Phoenix as well as the other projects."

"Sounds good, Tim."

CHAPTER 5

Championing Ideas

Tim sits in the coffee shop, going back and forth between staring at the blank wall and skimming through his resume for the umpteenth time. It is a contest between which one is more interesting. He heard about a project manager position for Software Dynamics and is wondering if it would be a good fit or not after he finishes his contract work for Randal and Gary. As Tim sees Randal pull into the parking lot, he puts away his resume.

"Hey Tim," sorry I'm a few minutes late," Randal mentions as he pulls up a chair.

"No worries, I'm just killing time. So Randal, how are things since our last TOC discussion?"

"Well not too good, Tim. Since we last talked a few things have happened. First between you and me, Micky, our interim CEO pulled a key staff meeting together and pretty much put a gun to our heads. He said we have to nail the next three contracts or we're going to be severely challenged in lining up our next round of funding. Which loosely translates to we could be out of business if we don't fix things ASAP."

"That sounds pretty serious."

"Exactly! Gary is working harder than ever to get his team to implement Critical Chain based on what you have been teaching us. But he needs results quickly. So I'm hoping you could step things up. Possibly get some compelling results in a week or two?"

© Eric Bergland 2016
E. Bergland, *Get it Done On Time!*, DOI 10.1007/978-1-4842-1860-0_5

Chapter 5 | Championing Ideas

"Umm Randal; it's not that simple. I really wish it was, but as with any process and culture change, it takes time to bring people up to speed, get their buy-in, and start implementing and changing behavior. I have been doing some training, but it takes time to set in."

"It isn't something we could quickly put together?"

Tim, realizing Randal is not really understanding how much time can be involved in implementing a new process, explains, "It takes time just advocating an idea and shepherding it through an organization. Let me give you an example of what it took for me to push what was supposed to be a simple idea through an organization. Sometimes it really needs passion and commitment to get something through. You need a champion." [frt 3]

LivingTV Interactive Company Background

One of the companies Tim worked for in the past was LivingTV Interactive. LivingTV Interactive was ahead of its time, but the concept was pretty clever. The basic premise is opposed to just watching TV, the company wanted you to be "Living it". The "Living it" aspect was due to interaction. This interaction with the show was handled by a combination of onscreen graphics displayed on the user's TV and a special remote. Most of the games broke into three major categories: sports, game shows, and dramas.

For sports, LivingTV Interactive would have someone in its studio watch the game and log every event into the system in real time. So if someone in a baseball game hit a ball, they would let the system know. If someone ran to a base they would let the system know. For the LivingTV Interactive players watching the game they would use the special remote to indicate if they thought the baseball player would hit the ball, strike out, take another base, or whatever. The system would then compare the LivingTV Interactive player's choice with the actual outcome in real time and score the player accordingly. The player that could best predict the events in the game would end up with the highest score and at the end of the game, their username would be shown for all to see.

LivingTV game shows and dramas were created in an entirely different way. To be able to create the LivingTV game, you needed to see the contents of the show before it aired. In this way you could create a game where LivingTV's players would play along with the game show contestants or ask them trivia about the show itself *while* it was airing. But to get access to the show and write about its contents *prior* to it being aired was challenging. You had to ask the TV show broadcasters to get access to the show before it aired and few broadcasters were willing to do this. The ones who were willing would charge very large fees. LivingTV Interactive, being a startup, was tight on cash and could only finance a small handful of basic shows for their subscribers. The major dramas and the associated huge audiences associated with them were far too expensive.

LivingTV Interactive's Dilemma

In working at LivingTV, Tim would often hear the same conversation over and over in LivingTV Interactive's hallways. The basic gist was the following...

If LivingTV Interactive put its limited resources into developing a *nationwide service* then it could attract the interest of major advertisers and in turn generate the revenues LivingTV needed to be profitable. The negative to this approach is that LivingTV would have a very broad nationwide market, *but* it would also have very limited programming options for its subscribers, as LivingTV could only support a few sporting events and a handful of drama and game shows.

The other approach was for LivingTV Interactive to put its limited resources into developing and paying broadcasting fees to increase the number of shows and *programs* it supports. This approach would provide depth to LivingTV's programming and would lead to multiple subscriber packages and a larger number of people subscribed in a given market. But with all the money invested in depth of programming only a limited number of markets could be addressed.

The arguments would then go back and forth. LivingTV Interactive simply did not have the funding to do both. It wanted a nationwide service to get more advertising, yet at the same time it needed to expand programming to generate more subscriber revenue in the markets it was in. Without a clear resolution or direction, LivingTV Interactive was simply *stuck*.

LivingTV Interactive's Conflict Cloud

Tim thought about the company discussions for a while—then it dawned on him. The discussions were really a conflict and Tim had the tool to try and find unique resolutions to conflicts, the TOC Cloud.

The first part was to draw out the cloud to help him visualize the conflict. It took about an hour to get all the wording right, but Tim was able to work through it and had sketched out the following diagram.

Chapter 5 | Championing Ideas

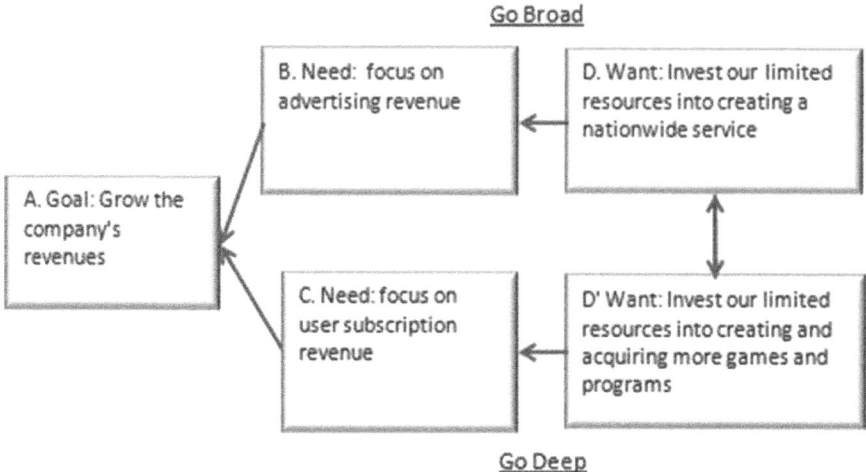

Everyone wanted LivingTV to grow and be successful so that was a *common goal* (A).

One side wanted LivingTV to invest its limited resources into creating a nationwide service (D). The *need* for this nationwide service was that by being nationwide we would have a market large enough to attract major advertisers that in turn would generate the revenues we wanted (B). This was the "Go Broad" strategy.

On the other side of the conflict was to invest our limited resources into creating and acquiring more LivingTV programs (D'). The reason was with more programs we could increase our subscriber reach and revenues for a given market (C). This was the "Go Deep" strategy.

The conflict was that there just was not enough money to do both strategies and people had ongoing disagreements about which strategy was better or they simply wanted to do both. The good part was now Tim was able to summarize, visualize, and look for ways to challenge and resolve the conflict.

Looking for Possible Resolutions

Based on the conflict cloud, Tim had three areas to challenge and see if he could find a resolution.

The first area was *the direct conflict* (D and D'). Was there a way to invest resources into both creating a nationwide service (D) and create more programs (D')? They could try and borrow enough money to do both, but that was unlikely. They could try and cut corners on both to spread the money around, but that really would not work well either.

Get it Done On Time!

The second was to look at the assumptions both sides were making. Tim looked to see if there were ways for LivingTV Interactive to reduce the cost of building a network (B D). Were there new technologies that could do more with less? Unfortunately no. Was there a way to deploy a low cost barebones LivingTV Interactive's service in more cities? Tim checked, no. Could LivingTV Interactive leverage someone else's existing infrastructure? No, nothing existed or could be modified to fit LivingTV Interactive's needs. At this time, their network was too specialized. Could LivingTV Interactive partner with another company and share the costs? Possibly. So some good thoughts, but nothing solid.

The last place Tim looked was to see if there was a way to get more programming in a less expensive way (C D'). Is there a way to get broadcasters to charge us less? Nothing apparent at this time. They either didn't care about LivingTV or just wanted the royalties. Would it be possible to partner with the broadcasters? It has been tried and there was just not much interest.

So overall the conflict held. Tim was able to better verbalize and challenge some of the conflict's assumptions, but he seemed just as stuck as everyone else.

Spark of an Idea

A few days later, Tim talked with Lori, one of the programming directors. "Lori, what limits LivingTV Interactive from doing more shows?"

"It depends on the show," responded Lori. "For sports, the events are done in real time. Since the show is publicly broadcasted, we do not need to pay for any royalties, so our costs are mainly around our people and equipment. The only issue is that there is no way for LivingTV Interactive to survive on just producing for the sports audience alone.

The segment our business really wanted was primetime dramas. It has huge audiences that we could tap into. To do that, we need to see the show in advance so we can create the LivingTV interactive script. To legally produce something in advance, we need permission from the broadcaster so we end up paying huge royalties. Since the royalties are based on the show's popularity, we can only do a handful of less popular day time dramas; forget anything in primetime. It's just too expensive for us."

"Isn't there a way to create a TV show script in real time like sports? After all if the TV show has been broadcasted you would not need to pay royalties," Tim asked.

"It has been looked at, but just did not make sense. There were just too many variables to try and do something on the fly. Certain events in sports are binary—either the player hits the baseball or does not. This does not translate as well over to dramas."

Chapter 5 | Championing Ideas

"What about having something right after a TV drama?"

"It's a nice thought Tim, but it takes a few hours to put together a good script for a show. By the time you have the script done, that show's audience is long gone."

Tim kept looking for ways to challenge the assumptions. "If we can't afford to pay to get all the dramas in advance, and we can't produce the dramas in real time, and it takes too long to create something for right after the TV drama, what is left?" Then it dawned on me pretty much every show is a weekly show. "Lori, what if we created a show that was based on the prior week's show. Then we could show it ten to fifteen minutes before this week's show. It would be a warm-up or pre-show before going into the main TV show. People could compete based on their knowledge of the show and last week's episode."

"Tim, given that it would shown right before next week's show, it would give us plenty of time to script out the show. Since it is based on an already broadcast show, the events in the show would be public domain so no royalties. Since we would not have to pay royalties, we pretty much could do as many shows as we want, even the primetime ones that we could not afford before. I think you might be onto something! Let me run it by my manager, if you can run it by yours, we'll see if there are any initial issues. We could also put together a proposal for your pre-show idea and run it by the weekly manager meeting."

Tim was feeling pretty good. He had hit upon the idea that might help break the organization's conflict. Going back and looking at his earlier cloud diagram, what assumption and connection did he actually break?

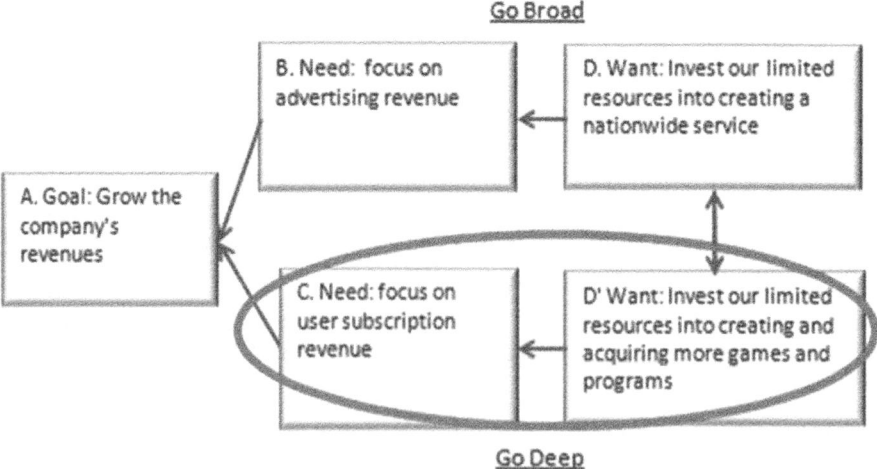

Get it Done On Time!

Tim's idea basically challenged the assumption that a LivingTV Interactive show has to be shown at the same time as the broadcast show. In looking at the diagram, *in order* for them to focus on user subscription revenues (C Need), *they must* invest resources into creating and acquiring more programs (D' Want). The underlying assumption was that there was no way to get programs without paying royalties. Tim challenged and broke this assumption with the what he called the *pre-show* concept. By building a game off a show already broadcast, LivingTV Interactive did not need the broadcaster's permission or to pay any royalties. LivingTV Interactive was free to develop as many shows as it needed (C Need) without needing to pay expensive royalties and thus would be able to focus its limited resources on building a larger market (B Need). Win win. Neither side (or need) of the LivingTV Interactive conflict loses out.

Initial Manager Meeting

Tim caught up with Mike, his manager, and gave him a quick run through of the concept. Mike felt pretty comfortable with it and agreed to add a quick 15-minute intro of the idea to the weekly manager meeting. Then Tim caught up with Lori and worked on the presentation. The only part left was to choose the snack that went with the presentation. LivingTV Interactive had a tradition of having a snack that related to the newest concept pitch. So for sports there were mini pretzels, for game shows there were animal crackers in the shape of letters (so you could spell things out). For the pre-show concept Lori and Tim agreed on Lays Potato Chips since they advertised that "you could not just eat one." Their hopes with the pre-show was that it was so fun that "you could not play just once."

At the meeting, people felt the pre-show idea had some potential. The "are we sure we can legally do this without getting sued" and "are we willing to do this" issue came up multiple times. Lori agreed to follow up with legal. The managers did agree that the concept was good enough so that it should be shown in the upcoming Exec review. There the goal would be to get approval to move forward with the idea to develop the concept and if approved, then on to the engineering development.

Tim was feeling pretty confident and thought after the Exec review, engineering could start working on the concept, but Lori was a little more cautious.

"Tim, getting the go-ahead to present in the Exec review is very good, but there is no guarantee. I've seen promising ideas proposed before only to have a few Execs hold out, ask for additional reviews, and basically drag out the approval process for months until people just give up. So take things with a grain of salt."

"Lori, that does not sound very encouraging. Do we know who the key people that are in the Exec review?"

"Pretty much. There is John who heads up my group, programming. Your manager Mike who heads up engineering, Bill heads up advertising, and Jim is the VP of operations. Those four are the key players. I'll talk with Terence in legal since we already have a copyright question. Human resources and IT are not involved in concept approvals, so we are okay there."

"Lori, I think I see your point. If we just give a 15-minute pitch in the Exec review where no one has seen or heard the idea before, we will get a whole bunch of questions, issues, and concerns that could cause the review process to drag out. What if we meet up with the key players before the Exec review? In this way, we can give them an overview, have them ask questions, and give us a little time to develop some answers to their concerns."

"Tim, that sounds possible. We can certainly meet with our managers. Bill is pretty approachable. Jim will be tough. His schedule is always booked."

Lobbying in Preparation for the Exec Review

Meeting with Lori's manager John, the head of programming, went pretty well. Overall he had been pushing for over a year to aggressively fund and expand the number of shows LivingTV Interactive supported. So anything that helped with his goal was an easy sell. The fact the pre-show concept did not require any royalties and could be created for any show was just ideal. The fact that the scripting team had a full week of real time to create the questions and interactions for each week's pre-show addressed his key logistical issues. Like everyone, he just had the concern about checking with legal.

The engineering meeting with Mike went pretty smoothly as well. He thought the idea was an interesting one. From a development perspective, the pre-show format followed similar games LivingTV Interactive had done, so he felt technically it should not be too hard to do, just a matter of getting approval. He asked Tim to review the idea with one of the senior engineers, Peter, just to get his take on it.

It took an hour of walking through the concept for Bill in advertising to understand how it all worked, but once he understood that a pre-show could be developed for any show and this could significantly increase the number of shows and programs LivingTV Interactive could support, Bill got excited. More shows meant a larger audience and more time with the audience. Even better, was prime time. With larger numbers, better demographics, and prime time, it would significantly boost Bill's opportunities to work with advertisers to sponsor and promote their products through LivingTV Interactive's network. Granted, LivingTV Interactive was available in only three cities at the moment,

Get it Done On Time!

but with more shows they could have much broader coverage in those cities and set up to expand from there.

The last person left was Jim, the VP of operations. In talking with his admin, Jim was regularly traveling to broadcasters, seeking venture capital, investors, and advertisers, trying to get support and investment money that kept LivingTV Interactive alive and going on a daily basis. He did not have an open spot for months. Yet he was also the most critical person.

Lori and Tim strategized for a while. They could just wait for the Exec review, but this was risky. Calling Jim without an appointment was out. They could try e-mailing him, but likely their e-mail would be lost. Then again, Tim thought if something stood out that caught his attention, it might get them the meeting they wanted. He looked at Lori and said he had it covered. "Let me double-check something and I'll get back to you." She looked a bit perplexed but decided to go along with it.

A few days later Tim got back to Lori and said they had a meeting next Thursday at 1 PM, Jim had a recent cancellation and wants to see what we have to show. Lori was floored.

"How did you get the meeting so quickly?"

"I'll tell you later," Tim coyly replied.

Thursday came around pretty quickly and Tim and Lori headed up to the third floor corner office. As they entered the office, the floor to ceiling windows offered amazing views of the LivingTV Interactive campus. Sunlight filled the room with warm light. Two paintings adorned the walls. Jim himself sat behind a large oak desk in an overstuffed recliner chair. It was quite a contrast from the grey engineering cubes and black ergonomic chairs three floors below.

"So… please come in. I'm anxious to see what you have to share," Jim said. "It's exceptionally rare that I get three e-mails all at the same time from my programming director, advertising director, and engineering director encouraging me to meet with someone. Usually they're busy arguing with each other over corporate strategy, funds, resources, and the like."

Lori looked over to Tim, "So that's how you got his attention to set up a meeting."

Tim smiled.

Tim and Lori spent about 20 minutes reviewing the pre-show concept. Jim nodded here and there and then looked over to them. "It's an interesting concept. I like the fact that it gives us the opportunity to produce any show and as many shows as we want without putting us through the ringer paying for royalties. We will have to double-check the royalty part with the lawyers of course. The other concern is that it is important for us to strategically align with broadcasters. We want them to see us as a way to leverage their content assets, not a parasite taking advantage of their work. Right or wrong, they could sue us out of existence if they wanted or cared. Let me mull this over. You have done a good job addressing my initial questions. We have an upcoming Exec review, so we can revisit the idea there. Thank you for putting so much work into this."

Meeting with Peter

Lori and Tim had about two weeks before the Exec review. Lori had already had a few meetings with the lawyers over the whole legality of the pre-show concept. Finding an identical case was proving unlikely given that LivingTV Interactive and its interactive service was a "never been done before" concept. Jim's major concern about being sued out of existence by the broadcasters if LivingTV Interactive was legally wrong was a bit haunting.

In the meantime, Tim decided to follow up with Peter, the senior engineer Mike had suggested. Tim reviewed the overall concept with Peter and he picked up on it pretty quickly.

"Tim, the pre-show interaction seems pretty straightforward," replied Peter. "We already have a scripting program for game shows. If we dropped some of the game show specific parts and focused on the trivia aspect of the pre-show, and simple interactivity, we could have a pretty quick prototype for your pre-show idea. So if you were able to get approval, I think it would take just a month to develop."

Tim thanked Peter for the insights and compared last minute notes with Lori as the Exec review approached.

Prep for the Exec Review

So there was one last item before the Exec review. Tim anxiously asked Lori about the legal status; it was one of the few things that could kill the whole pre-show concept.

"Legal got back to me," said Lori. "Basically they say it's our call. The shows themselves are copyrighted of course. But once the TV shows have been broadcast we can create trivia games asking our users what happened. For example, did John ask Jane out? How many times did Bill ask about the movie tickets, and so on."

"Sounds good, then I think we are ready."

"Agreed," said Lori.

The Exec Review

The time for the Exec review came and Lori and Tim finished up their last-minute preparations. As with the management meeting, there were plenty of Lays potato chips to go around.

Jim, the operations VP, went through a few key items and then went to the pre-show concept. "So are we ready to introduce the the pre-show concept?" He looked at the murmurings around. "Is anyone here not familiar with the pre-show concept?" No one answered. "Hmm, Tim seems like you and Lori have been busy and saved us some time. Does anyone have any open questions or concerns about the concept?" A few minor questions here and there, but basically it distilled down to the willingness to move forward with it. Jim sighed...

"I basically see it this way; we have been trying to get the broadcaster's interest for years. This concept gives us a chance to be able to expand our content and create interactive trivia shows for almost any TV program we want. I think it's worth the risk. On one side the broadcasters just ignore what we're doing. On the other side, we get their attention and it gives us a chance to discuss our company, possible partnerships, and advertising opportunities with them. All in favor of moving forward with a pilot show?" Everyone's hands went up to move forward.

Jim turned, "Mike how many months will it take to get this concept developed given the number of projects we currently have in the queue?" Mike looked over at Tim, "Tim, do you want to explain?"

"Jim, it's basically done," Tim happily stated.

"What do you mean, done?"

"In between our meeting and the exec review, Mike had me talk with Peter. Peter looked at an existing application initially. He thought it would take about a month to develop. He had a few days free about two weeks ago while he was having a project go through quality testing. He pretty much completed the pre-show concepts in a few days. He did not have to really code anything; he just stripped out a bunch of code from a prior game show project he had done before. Since quality assurance testing had already tested the original game show project, the pre-show just needed some simple sanity checking. We can start our first show next week if we want."

Both Mike and Tim smiled. Jim was surprised, "Impressive. Alright then. Let's get something on the programming schedule and start our first pilot next week. We can start with something small and then we can branch out from there."

The meeting finished shortly afterward. Lori looked over at Tim and said, "Good job."

Chapter 5 | Championing Ideas

Jim then pulled Tim aside. "Nicely done, Tim. You really went all out and did your homework. Usually, we spend weeks discussing and debating issues in the Exec review, but you addressed everyone's issues upfront so when we got to the Exec meeting, the main concerns were already resolved. It was just a matter of everyone seeing that they all agreed. You were even able to get a prototype up and running. I really appreciate the work you have done and hopefully it will help a great deal to make LivingTV Interactive a success."

The following week LivingTV Interactive started providing a pre-show for a primetime sitcom. It quickly became one of the most popular shows with LivingTV Interactive subscribers.

Back to Tim and Randal

"Well Tim, that is quite a story," states Randal. "You put a lot of work into developing the ideas and advocating for them."

"Yes, it was hard work. But also fun. Now imagine trying to do something more involved like changing the methodology of how an organization works."

"Actually Tim, it sounds a bit daunting," Randal says, letting out a deep breath. "Your story by itself was very involved. If we have to do that much work to implement Critical Chain into our environment is it even worth the effort? We don't have that much time to work with. And the list of items you are coming up with keeps growing and it is starting to sound impossible," Randal states with a touch of frustration.

"It's not so bad, Randal. There is a good amount of work involved. But it will have a real impact on the entire organization."

"I think you are being *idealistic* Tim," Randal a bit louder than he intended. "I know you want to help out, but do we really have to change the *whole* organization to get results? We need something simpler and quicker given our situation."

Tim ponders for a few minutes, then frowns. Sighing in resignation, "I think you are right Randal. Ideally we try to move the whole organization and culture, but like you said it can be a bit daunting and we're tight on time... Another approach is that we focus on one or two high-impact, high-value projects. We can get some good results and use that momentum and experience to help carry the rest of the implementation forward."

Perking up, Randal says, "That sounds much much better, Tim. Focusing on one project would be a lot simpler and a more reasonable given our time constraints. It would be much more doable. So how can we make this happen?"

"I'll set up a meeting with the three of us tomorrow. We can look at the implementation steps and as you noted focus on getting results out of the one project. I can work with Gary to train the team and build the schedules."

"Good Tim. You were worrying me there for a minute."

"So speaking of worry, just one more thing, Randal."

"Just one?" Randal says with a touch of concern.

"We still need to get the Exec buy-in. Gary is swamped in engineering details and even more so with putting Critical Chain into place. I need your help. Even though I have been working with some of the engineers, I'm still an outsider. Especially to the Execs. You have been with the company for several months, met and worked with the Execs, gained their respect, and built up some internal creditability. You have the visibility and influence across the different departments. I need you to help me work with and influence them. If they are not bought into the direction we are going, the whole implementation could quickly fall apart."

"Sounds a little challenging."

"But you want the company to succeed? Survive?"

Randal thinks for a moment. "They're good people, Tim. We will make it happen," Randal says with a smile… "We will definitely make it happen."

Future Reality Tree (FRT)

Tim ponders for a minute. To successfully implement Critical Chain we need to move the organization, on the other side we need to get early results to have momentum to move forward. Tim had always tried to move the whole organization first. In some cases, maybe it works better to work in a phased in approach with smaller steps.

"So any updates to your diagram?"

Tim looks up and sees Randal, "Just one for the FRT." Tim then takes out his Future Reality Tree and draws a box.

Chapter 5 | Championing Ideas

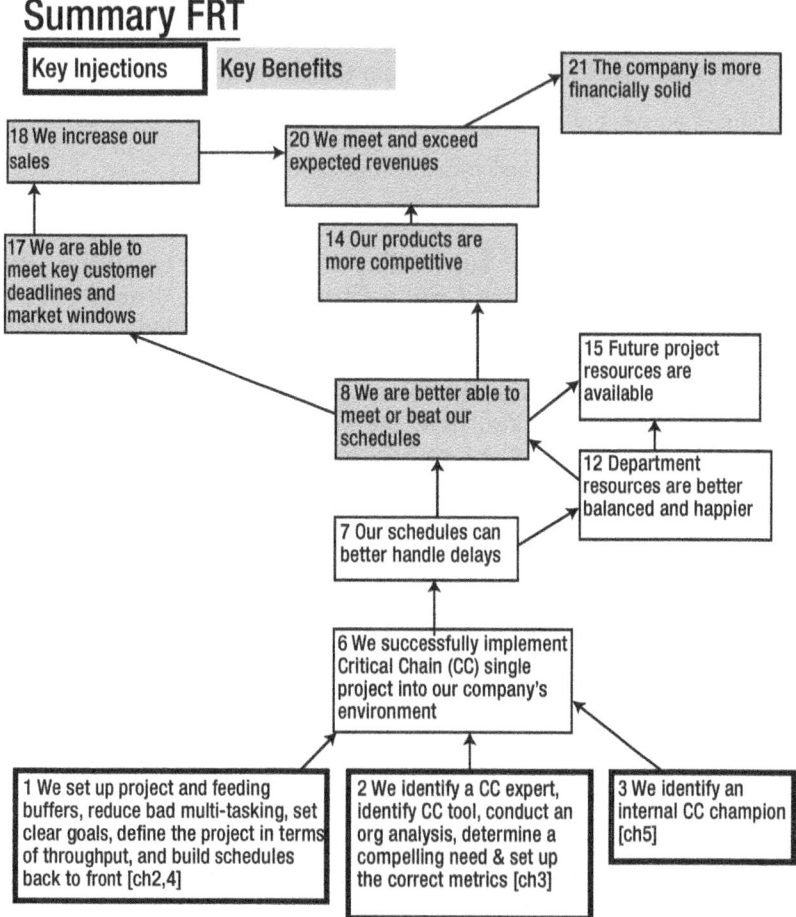

"So Randal, in order to 6) successfully implement Critical Chain we have to 1) implement the Critical Chain concepts, 2) be aware of the factors for successful implementations, and 3) identify an internal champion."

"Cool, since I am our company's internal TOC champion, I get my own box," says Randal.

"Sigh, I never quite thought of it that way, but yes, congratulations, you have your own box."

Current Reality Tree (CRT)
Core Conflict

Tim thinks for a few more minutes. "So Randal, at the base of the CRT is a core conflict. A central struggle that the organization is faced with. In the LivingTV Interactive example, their main conflict was between trying to go nationwide versus increasing the number of programs. So for our issues what is the core conflict driving the company? What are some of the conflicts we are seeing around the issues we are facing?"

"Well Tim, there is certainly ongoing tension between marketing and engineering. We could start there."

"Sure, can you explain it a bit more?"

"When I talk with Micky and Ashley about marketing, the focus is certainly on how to do more, go faster, and not lose quality. Micky wanted Exec reviews to ensure quality products were going out; he wanted to add urgent customer requests to the development schedules to show the customers that we can be responsive and attentive to the customer's needs; and he wanted to expand and add new products."

"Okay, that makes sense. So Randal, what is holding marketing back?"

Randal thinks for a moment, "Engineering I guess. They have only so many people and they are only able to get so much done, in fact it seems less and less of late."

"What is holding up engineering?" Tim thinks out loud for a moment. "The company is contractually obligated to deliver certain features and if marketing wanted future contracts then they needed to deliver a quality and innovative product on time. At the same time, the company needs to grow and take on new customers. Ahh…that is it!"

"What?" asks Randal.

"That is where the tension and conflict came from. With the company's current project-management process, we cannot meet current commitments *and* add new ones at the same time. Something has to give."

"I'm not completely following you, Tim."

"Here, it's like the LivingTV Interactive example," Tim then sketches out a few boxes, crosses them out, and then draws a few more. After a few minutes, he settles on one. "Here, I merged a few sample clouds together and created this. It might not be perfect, but it is good for now."

Chapter 5 | Championing Ideas

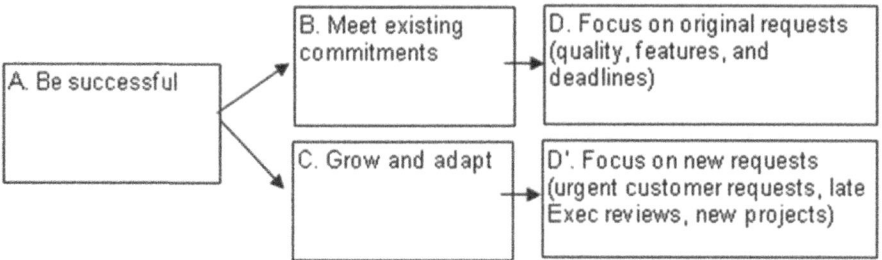

"So this is another conflict diagram thingy."

"More than that—it is *your* conflict cloud thingy." Not wanting to swamp Randal with too much theory, Tim asks, "Are you okay with this? The next few steps are a bit involved."

"Sure Tim. Pictures help and you certainly seem excited about it. And I'm now the champion so I might as well try and be familiar with what I can. Feel free to continue."

"So this cloud captures the struggle of your company. Everyone wants A) the company to be successful. On one side in order for A) the company to be successful, it must B) meet its existing commitments. In order to B) meet existing commitments, it must D) focus on the original requests. For example, engineering must work on the contracted features, deadlines, and quality expectations."

"Makes sense. The company needs to meet our current obligations."

"Correct Randal. At the same time in order for A) the company to be successful, it must C) grow and adapt. In order to C) grow and adapt, it must D') focus on new requests. For example, it must respond to urgent customer requests, make adjustments based on Exec reviews, and accept new projects."

"Ahh...this is the company and marketing needs to grow and expand the company."

"Yes, but it is struggling to do both."

"I kinda see it Tim. I mean every company needs to work on current needs *and* future needs. And I see that we are struggling a bit with that. But why would this be so compelling for us?"

"Hmm, let me redraw it as part of the bottom of the CRT. Like I said, if it is the true core conflict, you should see that it drives all the key issues you are facing."

Bottom of the CRT

Tim takes a few minutes and starts sketching and adding boxes to the CRT. He adds the boxes from the conflict and bolds their lines so they stand out. Then he sketches out some additional boxes at the base and bottom of the CRT diagram.

Summary Current Reality Tree Bottom

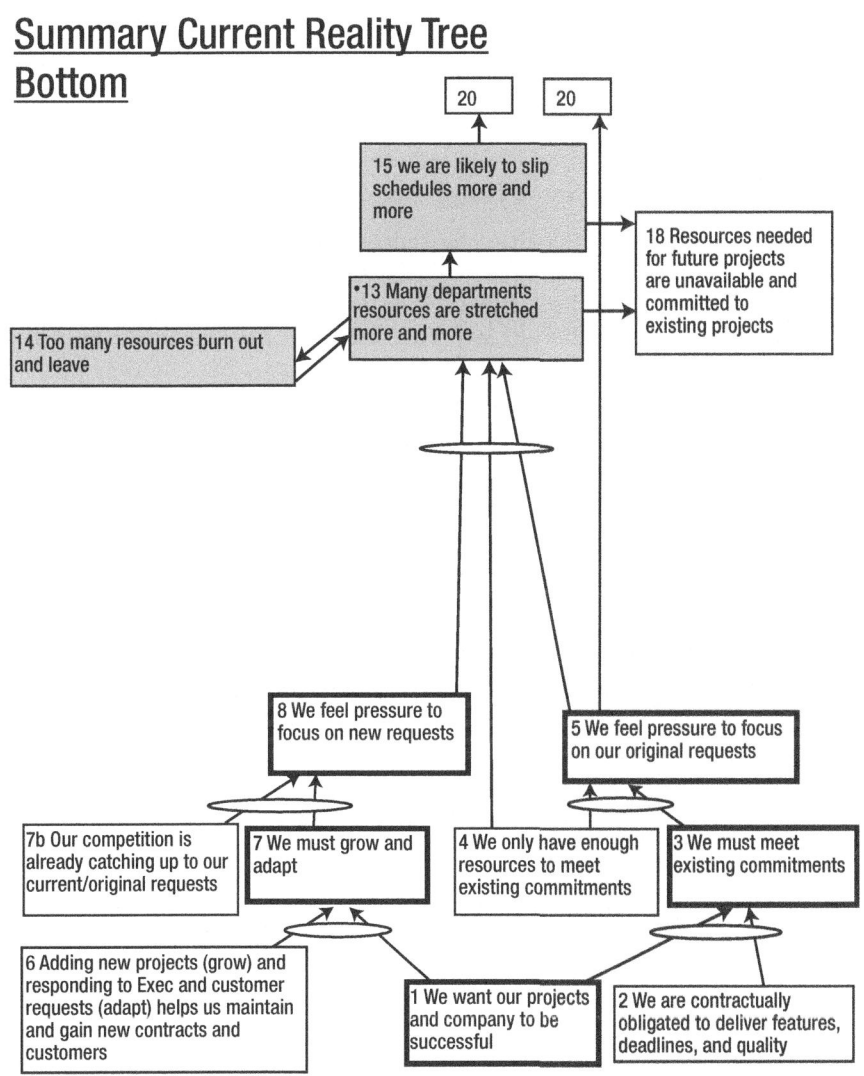

Chapter 5 | Championing Ideas

"Okay Tim, you added a whole bunch of boxes. Care to elaborate?"

"So I added the core conflict to the bottom of our CRT diagram. The bold boxes relate to the cloud we just talked about. The other boxes add more clarity. So if we 1) want to be successful and 2) we are obligated to meet our contractually agreements with customers (deliver specific features, on-time and of high quality) then the company must 3) focus on meeting our existing commitments. If we must 3) meet existing commitments and 4) we only have enough resources to meet our existing commitments, then 5) we must focus our efforts on meeting our original requests."

"Makes sense. This is the area Gary and engineering struggles with—meeting existing commitments. And he always talks about wanting more resources. So yeah, I can see that he has some struggles there. So what next?"

"At the same time if we 1) want to be successful and 6) adding new projects (grow), responding to Exec and customer requests (adapt) helps us maintain and gain new contracts and customers, then 7) we must grow and adapt. If we 7) must grow and adapt, then 8) we must focus on new requests. But why? Sure Micky and marketing wants to grow the company, but are they pushing impossibly hard?"

"I can answer that one, Tim. Part of it is that Micky wants to make his mark, but even more so Micky feels that the company has fallen farther and farther behind and that the competition will overtake us. Once that happens, the competition will start pulling away critical and long-term contracts that have sustained our company. He feels we have to keep growing to ensure our survival."

"Ahh, that makes a lot more sense. So in order to 7) grow, we must 8) focus on new requests because 7b) the competition is catching up and putting the entire company at risk. This helps to explain why Micky is so driven."

"Yep."

"Randal, it also explains that Gary and the company must be under intense and impossible pressure. On the one side, everyone is trying to 5) meet current expectations at the same time 8) there is all this pressure to focus on new requests and 4) we only have enough resources for the original requests. So we either focus on one or the other or oscillate between the two and do neither particularly well."

"And that is why engineering is not only struggling with the original contracts, but they are falling more and more behind. They are getting pulled into growth work as well."

"But the current product development system can't support both areas. So 8), 4), and 5) all lead to 13) many departments resources are stretched more and more and the problems get worse and worse."

"I think you need to rename your CRT the doom cloud. It doesn't paint a very pretty picture."

"True and if I keep talking theory we're going to be in trouble," Tim says, thinking back to the LivingTV Interactive layoffs all over again. Too little, too late. "Randal, we need to get moving."

CHAPTER 6

High-Level Implementation Steps

Tim sits patiently waiting for Randal. Sighing, he looks out the window. The grey skies cast long shadows in the company parking lot. The raindrops slowly gather into puddles. Randal enters the company café, shaking out his umbrella and taking off his rain coat. Gary follows Randal in shortly thereafter. Tim checks his watch—only two minutes late, which is not too bad for Randal.

"So Tim," Gary says, sighing very heavily and looking at Tim, "Micky is putting even more pressure on us. Before you started, we promised to make changes to improve the Griffin project, but it is looking like the results are not going to be very good and we are running into the same issues our past projects have run into—despite all the changes we tried to make. We need to put this Critical Chain approach into place quickly."

"I was discussing the same thing with Tim yesterday!," states Randal. "We determined that we need to pick one or two top projects, focus our efforts there, and then use the early results to convince management."

© Eric Bergland 2016
E. Bergland, *Get it Done On Time!*, DOI 10.1007/978-1-4842-1860-0_6

"Umm," Tim says, stepping in. "Just a quick note on that. Ideally we try and move the whole organization for a Critical Chain implementation. If time is an issue then we can look at staggering the implementation and pick one or two high-impact projects to focus on. They need to have a bottom line impact as well and cannot be side projects since the effort needed and results created would not be taken seriously."

"Does it have to be a new project, Tim?" inquires Gary. "We have Phoenix that has been in development for the last two months. The next new project starting up will be in three months."

"Given the time constraints, I think we're going to have to intercept Phoenix," Tim suggests.

"Timeline-wise I agree it makes sense, but Tim, I can't afford to have the whole team stop work and pull them into a network build."

"I see your point, Gary. Do you know the Phoenix schedule pretty well?"

"Between myself and Jeremy the Phoenix project manager, we know it inside and out," says Gary.

"Then the three of us could work on the schedule offline, pull some of the key info from the teams, and then when it looks okay, review it with them. It would be better if they were involved in creating it and would have more ownership, but this is the next best alternative I could think of."

"That is workable, Tim. We need results and the Griffin post mortem is in a few days. I don't want to be standing there saying that we are going to use the exact same approach for Phoenix when Griffin did not go so well."

"Tim, just a quick note," interjects Randal. "If we focus all of the resources and attention on Phoenix, won't it just look like we are sacrificing the other projects to make this one look good?"

"Hmm, I see your concern, Randal. We will be working with the existing resources. The only part we are changing is the methodology. But you are correct that we will have to manage the perception as well as having the managers agree on the priority of the different projects. We will also need to bring the key stakeholders up to speed. Gary, other than the project team and yourself, who else is involved in how the projects are set up and run?"

"Mainly it is my area of expertise. But Grant, the Chief Operating Officer, and Micky still need to sign off on it. I already have given them a heads up that we're looking into something new, but it would be good if you could provide a more detailed overview."

"Sure, I can work with Randal and set up some meetings with them next week. Are you up for it, champ?"

Randal looks over at Tim, "So you have given me about a day to get settled into this internal champion role you have created?"

"Pretty much. We can review the high-level concepts with the Execs [Chapter 2] and review the detailed concepts with the Phoenix project team [Chapter 4]. I have also been working on the TOC organizational analysis so I can share what I have so far with you as well. Don't worry...I can lead the discussions, but you should be there for some of them just to see how I go through the process."

"Fair enough, Tim," Randal says contently.

"So Gary and Randal, just one last thought. To really make a culture change in an organization, we need three things:

- Top management buy-in and agreement to lead the charge.
- Determine key measurement changes that will incentivize the desired behaviors of the new culture.
- Education for all involved. The education includes the new measurements. (Bibliography 1)

Gary, you are already leading the development efforts. Randal and I can follow up with Grant and Micky. So that should help us cover the first point. I will cover metrics in just a few minutes when we talk about how to manage the schedule. And lastly the education..."

"Tim and I will handle the Exec reviews and team training," Randal injects.

"What?" looking at Tim, "you said you wanted me to work more closely with you. So I can't finish your sentences?"

Tim just rolls his eyes. "Come on Gary. We have a schedule network build to start on for Phoenix."

Phoenix Network Build

Gary takes Tim over to meet the Phoenix project manager's cube. "Tim, I would like you to meet Jeremy. He has been with us for about two years now and has a very good handle on the Phoenix project."

Tim looks over at Jeremy. He is a young 30-something engineer with dark hair and a few grey hairs starting to creep in. "It is nice to meet you, Jeremy. Has Gary talked with you about Critical Chain and what we need to do?"

"Not so much," replies Jeremy while looking over at Gary a bit cautiously.

"Well, it looks like we will need to give you a crash course. Is there a conference room we could use for a while?"

"Sure."

Chapter 6 | High-Level Implementation Steps

From there, Tim and Gary bring Jeremy up to speed on the company's situation, the issues with Griffin, how they need to do something different, and why they want to target his project to show results. Tim also provides a summary of the key Critical Chain concepts [Chapters 2 and 4]."

Jeremy looks over at Gary, "So Gary, you are the VP of engineering and you are signing off on this?"

"Yes."

"And you are okay that we are adding more risk and potential delays by changing our process during the execution?" Jeremy cautiously asks Gary.

"If we stick with what we did for Griffin, we're likely to get the same results."

"Agreed. I just wanted to be sure I have your signoff. Okay, a new process it is. Sounds pretty cool. So Tim, where do we start?"

"Jeremy, we need to start with a clean slate, but we can quickly pull in items from the prior schedule. As I noted in the review, we need to clarify our project goal and make sure it is clear, measureable, and has a timeframe."

"Sure Tim, already done."

"Next we need to drive the project to throughput, where we actually generate revenue."

"That is an interesting question, Tim. Typically we count the product as done when we finish QA and make the software available to the customer to download," explains Jeremy.

"Tim," Gary interjects, "Phoenix is custom software. Per the contract we set up, we actually do not receive payment at that time. The customer has to actually download the software, integrate it into their environment, and confirm it is functional per the features and specs promised in the contract. Only then do we get paid."

"Okay, Gary, then that is where the project ends. We need to include the customer integration and signoff that is feature complete per the contract as part of our schedule."

Jeremy looks over to Gary. "You okay with this? It will really stretch out the timeline of the project."

"But hopefully Jeremy it can shorten the time it takes us to complete the project and get paid," responds Gary.

"Ahh, that would be good."

Tim then looks over to Jeremy, "How often do you do software drops to the customer?"

"We have ongoing discussions and clarifications with the customer, but typically they do not get the actual software until we are done. So we spec out the product, develop it, test and fix issues, and deliver. Some products are just six to eight months."

"Jeremy, have you tried sharing early versions of the software with the customers earlier?"

"It has been problematic, Tim. It triggers a ton of changes. That is why we spend so much time upfront on the specs. That way when the development and testing is done, we can safely say the development is complete."

"Have there been customer issues when the product has been delivered?," asks Tim.

Jeremy looks over to Gary. "Ongoing issues, Tim. There are always items that come up even though the provided solutions line up to the spec."

"And does this delay payments, Gary?"

"Pretty much. Sometimes we're rushed so it is not an ideal implementation; sometimes the customer gets what they asked for and spec'ed, but they really intended something else. If they are important enough and complain enough Micky will have us rework some areas just to pacify the customer and so we can get paid."

"Jeremy if we are building the project out to throughput and where we get actually paid, we might want to consider some early customer drops and reviews to customers. They will likely have some issues and changes, but you can negotiate them during development as opposed to the customer stalling payments."

"I can see where you are going with this, Tim. It is not easy, but in theory it could reduce some of the issues we have once the customer gets the software. So we could certainly try it."

"I will also be sure to include the contracts team in the discussions. If the customer tries to change something mid-project, we will need to negotiate it," Gary adds.

From there Tim, Jeremy, and Gary look at the revised goal and worked backward using the phrasing *in order to.. we must…* They add in dependencies, build out the schedule, and leverage the items that were created in the original schedule, just as Tim had shown Gary before [Chapter 4]. For each task, Gary and Jeremy assign a resource and provide the unbuffered focus time as well as the 90% confidence low-risk duration.

"I think it looks like a pretty good network for a first pass," states Gary.

"It's huge," Jeremy remarks. "Micky would never go for this."

"It's okay Jeremy," Tim replies. "It's the first pass. Now we need to scrub the schedule. Since we already did a backward pass, let's do a forward pass *if I have everything at first task then is there anything else I need before I can work on the second task?*"

Tim, Jeremy, and Gary talk at look at the schedule's PERT or network view to see and check the tasks and dependencies and proceed to walk through the schedule from beginning to end.

"Tim, why is the Critical Chain tool staggering this set of tasks? There is no dependency?"

"Hmm, good question, Jeremy. Critical Chain resolves resource contentions. It looks like Jim is doing this entire set of tasks. Since he cannot do them all at once, the Critical Chain tool staggered them."

"That isn't right though. Jim is the lead for that area and he has plenty of people on his team to do the work."

"So is Jim is not the resource doing the work?"

"No Tim, not at all. Jim is responsible for assigning resources to work on that area. That is why we assigned his name to those tasks."

"For Critical Chain, that is not going to work. We need the actual resources or possibly a resource pool assigned, not the manager. Since these tasks are resource-driven, the more resources we can have work in parallel, the more we can compress the overall schedule."

"Fair enough Tim, it's an easy fix." And with that Jeremy updates the schedule accordingly.

Tim is wary of additional managers in the schedule and so he scans for more tasks staggered by resource available versus actual dependencies. He zeros in on another area. "So, why are so many of these tasks with Amy staggered due to resource contention? Is she a resource manager also?"

"No Tim," Jeremy indicates, "She is one of our top user interface designers. When we need something critical done really well she is the go-to person and people often ask for her to work on certain areas specifically."

"That is fine up to a point. But when you look at this part of the schedule, you can see her availability is stretching out the timeline. Is she the only user interface designer, Jeremy?"

"No, not at all. Jenny has ramped up since Griffin and has gotten pretty good."

"So could we have Jenny cover some of these tasks where Amy is resource constrained? It would help us compress our schedule that much more."

Jeremy thinks for a moment, "Sure Tim, it's workable."

The team then goes back to the schedule once more.

"Jeremy, why is this sequence of tasks significantly longer than this parallel sequence? From my experience, they should both take about the same time," inquires Gary.

"I added some additional time into the focused estimates for the first sequence. I figured that it is a newer task for the team and a bit riskier."

"You need to be careful Jeremy," states Tim. "We don't want to add padding and safety time back into the focused durations. If you are concerned about risk, add time to the low-risk duration. In that way you will add more time to the feeding or project buffer to account for the risk and at the same time you will not unnecessarily stretch out the schedule."

"Okay Tim. I recall you mentioning that point; just trying to get the hang of actually implementing it."

"No problem. It takes some practice."

From there they continue to go through the schedule and Tim pushes them to challenge several other dependencies and look for additional ways to make more items in the schedule parallel. After a while and a few challenging discussions, they have significantly compressed the schedule.

"So Tim, it looks like we are almost there. Any other network building tricks you might have?"

"Sure Jeremy, the last item I have is BORA (Bibliography 2)."

"BORA?"

"Break a link, Overlap tasks, Reduce scope or duration, or Add a resource. In short, BORA. So we can review the Critical Chain and see if these can help us. Would breaking a dependency allow us to do more work in parallel? Does one task have to completely finish before the successive task starts? If not, we could overlap them. In looking at the tasks, can we reduce scope or duration? And lastly, are there tasks that if we added more resources to them, could they finish faster?"

"It's an interesting question, Tim. We can do yet one more pass just in case your BORA can help us get to where we need to be."

They begin working and then after about 20 minutes Jeremy inquires, "So Tim, the schedule is looking better, but one more question."

"Sure, Jeremy."

"You say the project buffer is at the end of the project and we build the project all the way out until we get paid. At the same time per contract we have a solid delivery date to provide the final software drop. We can't miss this date, but it is not protected by the project buffer."

"Very good question. For those cases, we can use something called a *buffered end point*. So for the main schedule all the tasks have to tie together and to a project end task. For the delivery we can set up a separate task for this deliverable without any successive tasks. The Critical Chain tool will automatically create a separate buffer just for this milestone."

From there, Tim and Jeremy meet with the project team. Tim provides a high-level overview of Critical Chain [Chapter 2]. Then he and Jeremy walk through the schedule and the estimates with them and make minor adjustments as needed. Overall the teams were good with the schedules, liked the project buffers, but were wary of the unbuffered focus times and being held to them.

Phoenix Execution

"So once the schedule has been built, we have three areas we focus on for execution: buffer management, recovery, and behaviors. For each end point in the schedule, there is a project buffer and for each project buffer we can check its fever chart." Tim reaches into his computer bag and pulls out the following diagram.

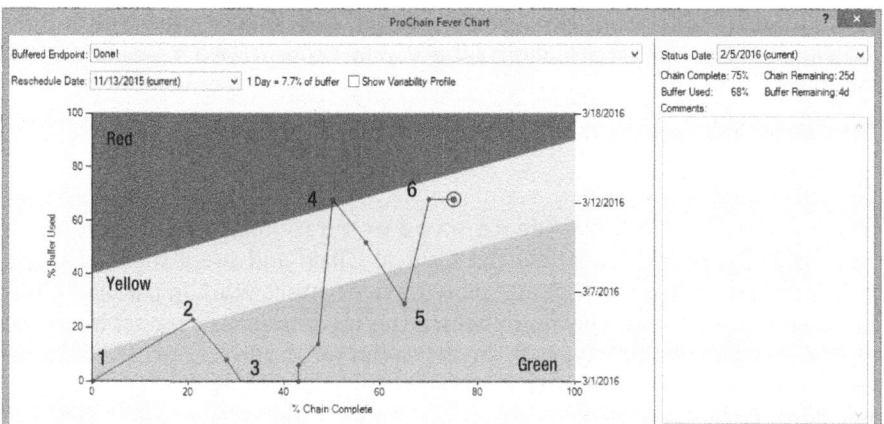

"Here is a fever chart for a simple and short sample project. So there are three main colors: green, yellow, and red. After each schedule update, typically weekly, we need to review the fever charts. The fever charts tell us how far into the project buffer we are as well as how quickly we are using it."

"Tim, can you explain the red, yellow, green zones a bit more?" inquires Jeremy. "Your Critical Chain overview with me did not cover this."

"Sure, each color relates to the amount of project buffer left in relation to how far we are into the project (or Critical Chain completed). So as you can see with updates and points 1-3 we have consumed some of the project buffer,

Get it Done On Time!

but in relation to our progress we are in the green and doing okay. Then with point 4 you can see we hit a major challenge, used a good amount of time in the buffer, and did not make much progress on the Critical Chain."

"So what did you do in this case?" inquires Gary.

"Well, being in the red, we knew the overall project deadline was at risk yet we still had a fair amount of time left in the project. So we went back and looked at BORA to find ways we could *recover*. In this particular case we were lucky and could just add an additional resource to help out with a few key tasks. That allowed us to recover and get back on track. So as you can see with update 5 we were back in the green."

"But Tim, point 6 is in the yellow."

"Correct, with the schedule being short and the project buffer so small you will see the fever chart go up and down more quickly. With a larger project and larger buffer, we should see it go up and down more gradually pending any major issues. In the case of point 6, we are in yellow. So we are not late, but we are at risk of being late. So we have reviewed the remaining tasks to see what steps we can take to move us back to yellow or to green pending any additional issues."

"So Tim, if I understand you correctly, the project buffer serves as a bank of time. Using the fever chart, we can see if we have enough time reserved to protect our overall deadline based on where we are in the project."

"Correct, Jeremy."

"So we covered the mechanics of managing the project buffer. The next part we need to cover is the behaviors we need during execution. For example, we are managing the resources to the unbuffered focus times and aggregating the safety time into the project buffer. So we expect the resource to be late on some tasks."

"But Tim, if we let the resources go too late, it could put the schedule at risk."

"Jeremy, we want to be sure we are managing the project against the overall deadline. If we beat up resource for minor delays, especially when they are working to unbuffered dates, they will start putting time back into the tasks and that will in turn stretch the schedule out more and more."

"Tim, this is a bit different than what I'm used to."

"No problem Jeremy, we can set up some simulations and practice exercises and so you can get a better feel and get more comfortable with it. To help us keep moving forward, we want to be sure to encourage *roadrunner* and *relay race* behaviors."

"Tim, can you elaborate a bit more?"

Chapter 6 | High-Level Implementation Steps

"Sure Jeremy, like in the concepts review [Chapter 4], we want resources to start working on a task as soon as they get it, so that's roadrunner. We also want to make sure resources hand off completed work to the next resource as quickly and smoothly as possible, so that's the relay race."

"Okay, makes sense Tim. Maintain forward momentum; try to minimize task delays."

"Correct, and in addition we want to avoid and minimize bad multi-tasking and student syndrome."

"Clarity please; you're introducing a whole new vocabulary," Jeremy says with a smile.

"Student syndrome is short for people being deadline driven and waiting until the last minute to work on something. As noted we want them to start as soon as possible—roadrunner. Bad multi-tasking is where people work on too many things at once and in turn it causes all of the work to stretch out. I can walk you through more examples if you want [Chapter 4]."

"I think I'm good for now. I think doing the practice exercises and getting some hands-on experience with this will be more critical. I'm seeing lots of little pieces. Is this captured anywhere?" inquires Jeremy.

"The team training and exercises will cover the same items. I am also working on a document that will capture the prior issues and the new direction we are going (CRT/FRT). I will have it done shortly and can review it with you if you want."

"That would be good, Tim. So are we done?"

"One last item."

Phoenix Post-Mortem Plan

"Jeremy and Gary, the last item I just wanted to note was POOGI, which stands for the Process Of OnGoing Improvement. So we have set up Critical Chain to help address some of the organization's key issues. Once we implement it, the issues the organization will face will change. We just need to be aware of that and note that we need to work to improve our process to be more effective and efficient."

"Seems very Agile-like?" states Jeremy.

"True, several different methodologies say similar things. Mainly don't get complacent. Don't rest on your laurels."

"We do regular post-mortems at the end of our projects," Jeremy indicates. "I have been thinking that it would be good to do a review after each major milestone. Given that this is a new process for the team, a more frequent review would be valuable."

Get it Done On Time!

"Good idea, Jeremy. I think you are onto something. So Gary, I can work with you, Jeremy, and the team on the Critical Chain training and exercises. I'll also work with Randal to schedule some meetings with the Execs. For me and you is there any other area you need my help on?"

"We have the Griffin post-mortem coming up. I think it would be good for you to listen in, Tim, and see some of the issues we have run into the past and then see what adjustments you might want to make so we can be more successful with Critical Chain."

"Sounds good, Gary. I will be there."

Micky's Urgent Requests

Tim hesitates for a minute, "So Gary and Jeremy, before we leave I just wanted to touch base on something I have been hearing about."

"Yes Tim?" Gary inquires.

"Can you tell me a bit more about these urgent customer requests and late Exec reviews?"

"It's a new thing Micky started once he became the interim CEO," states Gary. "He has been pushing to get more contracts and more out of the contracts we have. As part of this, he has been trying to build out the products and make engineering more responsible. Is that your sense Jeremy?"

"Some, Gary." Jeremy says, looking a bit frustrated. "His goals make sense. But it has also lead to Micky trying to sneak extra work and urgent customer requests [crt 11] into our projects without changing the deadlines. We typically call this *scope creep*. We keep trying to push back, but he has taken it more as defiance than understanding and it is making meeting our schedules more challenging."

"Don't you use a change control process?" inquires Tim. "Basically once execution starts, any new requests have to be reviewed and assessed for schedule impact. If it's a large enough change, then new resources have to be added, features traded off, timelines changed, and contracts adjusted and/or it is simply added to the next release."

"We have a process, Tim." Gary replies somewhat frustrated. "Just Micky chooses to ignore it from time to time."

"So Gary, these requests complicate and delay the project?"

"Correct Tim. Micky doesn't want to hear it, but yes it does impact the schedules."

"What about the late Exec reviews?" [crt 10]

Chapter 6 | High-Level Implementation Steps

Gary sighs. "Yeah, that is another thing Micky recently added. He wants to make sure we're releasing a quality product. He does not believe in PowerPoint presentations since the actual software could look and work much differently. So he wants to see the actual product."

"He also does not want to see buggy alpha code or module development," Jeremy adds. "He wants to see it as complete as possible. Sometime between beta and gold release he wants a demonstration. So while we are in the final stretch of development, I have to have engineers work on presentations. Worse than that, Micky regularly has changes he wants made in these meetings. So we have to scramble to try and include his adjustments in addition to all of the other final software coding that needs to be done."

"Hmm, it sounds a bit challenging to me," states Tim, concerned.

"It is, Tim. Our schedules were already tight [crt 16] before all of this. Now we have to add customer requests and late Exec requests to other delays and issues and we're prone to have problems hitting our deadlines with the features we're contractually required to deliver," Jeremy adds.

"And talking to Micky about this?" inquires Tim.

"Again, he doesn't want to hear what he feels are engineering excuses," states Gary. "He wants us to be nimble and more responsive."

Tim thinks for a minute. "Ideally, we could get Micky to better understand and possibly back off a bit, but that does not seem easy. It would be better if we could be more disciplined with our change control policies [frt 9]."

"It would be a miracle if you could get better change control. A much needed miracle," states Gary.

Thinking a bit more, "If I can't get Micky to reduce the Exec changes what if we just reserved some of the development capacity instead. Gary, you know urgent requests are going to come in and you know Micky will make changes. So just plan it in."

"It's a bit tricky, Tim. We don't know what the changes will be. But I see where you are going with it. It's too late for our Griffin project, but maybe in the Phoenix project it's something we could look at." Gary feels a bit more optimistic. "It doesn't solve the problem, but it could at least help us better manage it. Jeremy, could you look at the schedule and possibly work this in?"

"Sure Gary, I'll work on it right away. I'll add it in as management changes so it does not look like we're just trying to pad the schedule"

"I'll chat with Randal and see how we want to go about working with Micky. Instead of directly confronting him about the problems with the urgent requests and late Exec reviews, possibly we could work around it to better support his and the company's needs." It is not ideal, but just maybe it could work, thinks Tim.

CRT

As Gary and Jeremy leave, Tim drops Randal a quick IM. "Working on the CRT and FRT; are you still interested?"

"Sure. Be over in a minute" Randal replies.

Tim then takes out his CRT diagram and sketches in a few more boxes.

Summary Current Reality Tree Bottom

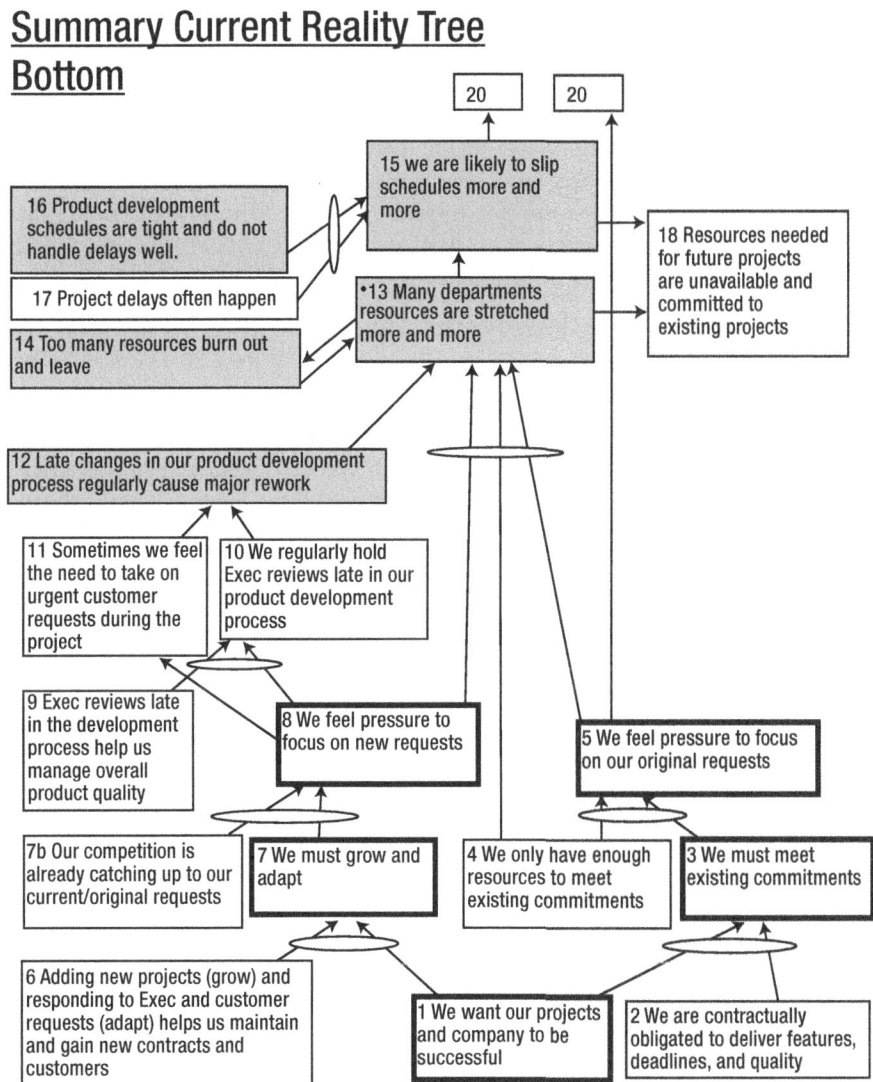

Chapter 6 | High-Level Implementation Steps

"So sketching in more boxes, I see. Your shrub has started to grow into a tree," Randal says as he enters the room.

"Yes it has. Some of it relates to marketing. So I thought you would be interested."

"Sounds good."

"So I was working with Gary and Jeremy. The first two boxes are simple, as we know 16) product development schedules are already tight and 17) project delays can often happen. This by itself can lead to 15) schedules slipping."

"Makes sense, but it's good to highlight the issue since it's a significant concern for us."

"In addition to this, I added a few items from the "grow the company" side. First 9) and 10) we regularly hold Exec meetings late in the development process and 11) sometimes we get urgent requests. These lead to 12) late changes in our development process that cause additional rework that leads to 13) stretching out our departments."

"Interesting, Tim. I know Micky wants those changes to grow the company and wants to be sure we are not letting quality slip. But the way you have it drawn here it also highlights the added pressure engineering is under."

"Exactly. There are good reasons for the changes, but we can also see the tension and looking at the rest of the CRT we can see the consequences coming out of it. I just need to get some additional Exec feedback and I should have a pretty complete picture of our overall challenges. Then with the FRT I will be able to show a solid way to move forward."

"Part of your master plan, Tim?"

"Pretty much. Critical Chain by itself can help cover some items, but, yes, with the overall plan I can see what else is needed and why."

FRT

Tim then takes out the FRT diagram he has been working on and adds a few more boxes.

Get it Done On Time!

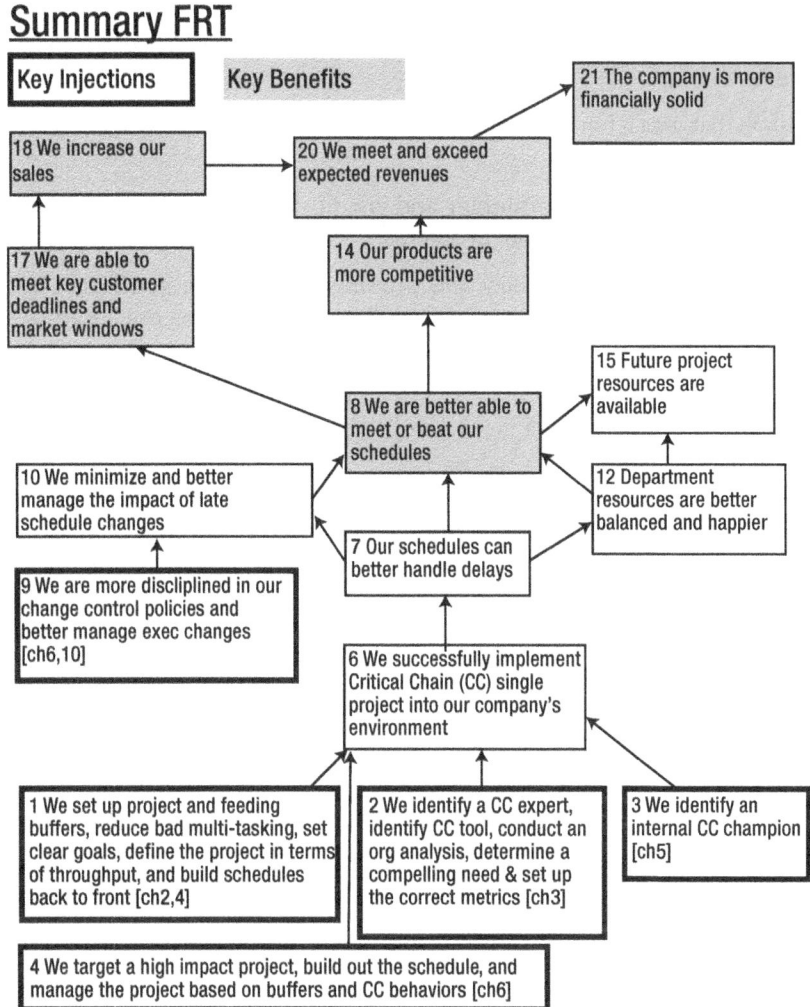

"So Randal, just a few items here. The first is the meeting I just had with Jeremy and Gary where 4) we focus on a high-impact project, build out the schedule, and *manage* (not just set up) the project based on buffers and CC behaviors."

"Sounds better, Tim. We have talked a good amount about concepts. If we want results, we need to start implementing. So good to hear that this is moving along."

"The other two items are 9) and 10) we need to be more disciplined in our change control and better manage Exec changes if we 8) want to keep our schedules."

"I am sure that was a fun discussion with Gary and Jeremy. Micky and marketing will likely push back."

"True. But we have to do something and just putting in Critical Chain without addressing this won't solve our problems."

"Well Tim, I can talk with Gary and possibly Grant. The good part is that I have confidence that with your help, we'll figure something out," Randal says with a smile.

CHAPTER 7

Using Ambitious Targets to Handle Past Issues

Tim sits quietly as Micky the interim CEO spends three hours talking over the Griffin project post-mortem and ripping into the poor results and anyone he felt was responsible. Rushed release, faulty code [crt 20], frustrated and lost customers [crt 27], and below expectation revenues [crt 26] were his key criticisms. The Griffin project manager looked sheet white, ready for a firing squad and his impending demotion.

Micky zeroed in on Gary, the engineering manager. "You need to fix this! We cannot afford these types of mistakes and hope to survive. I want a report next week on how you are going to improve this. Change something, fire someone, or get something out of that new consultant you hired. We cannot do this again!" Micky storms out of the room. Everyone sits quietly.

© Eric Bergland 2016
E. Bergland, *Get it Done On Time!*, DOI 10.1007/978-1-4842-1860-0_7

Gary looks nervously over at Tim. "Tim, I am going to finish talking with the software engineers. Can you talk with QA and see how we let so many issues go out to our customers?"

"Sure Gary," replies Tim.

Tim walks over to the QA offices, anxious to let the intensity of the prior meeting cool off. Once there, he found the QA leads Anthony and Nir. Anthony is a rather burly guy. Nir is a bit lean, bald, and definitely looks tired and worn out.

"Hi Anthony and Nir. I am working with Gary to help improve his project management process," states Tim.

"We need it. I heard Micky crashed the engineering review meeting guns blazing," Nir replies. "I figure the next place people he is looking to blame is QA."

"So can you give me a little background on your QA process?" Tim asks, not trying to get too caught up in Nir's soap box.

"Sure. Whatever. I just finished the Griffin project, the one that just exploded. We worked like mad to finish that with the time they gave us. Anthony over here is in the process of developing the base test plan for the Phoenix project."

"And how are these test plans put together?" inquires Tim.

"We've reviewed the initial feature spec, broken out the key areas, and then detailed the various functional tests and test cases to exercise," Anthony replies. "Once the engineers get further along in their coding, we should be able to do some initial testing. And then at the end of the project, it's the final testing phase."

"So you feel that we are in pretty good shape?"

"It's the tried and true process we've been using for a while."

Nir is tired and overly frustrated and he reflexively interjects, "We had a pretty good plan going into Griffin too! The engineers *always* kill us in the end! We had set up our test plans, ramped up our testing teams, and had our test systems all ready. We planned a standard two-month test cycle for the final testing phase. Engineering just could not give us stable code that worked. At first we just could not get anything for weeks. Then when we received the early code and it just crashed so there just was not much to test. By the time engineering had something that did not blow up right away, we had a little more than two weeks left. We complained like crazy, but we were talking to a wall. The client had a drop-dead date, so it was not like we could push out the schedule. The engineers were working like crazy and since it took longer than expected, they took all the time out of the QA schedule. So we did very little testing and shipped out an extremely buggy and poor-quality product [crt 20]. So as far as our plan on paper right now, we look fine. But if engineering is late as it usually is, the plan goes out the window. In fact, the last few projects engineering ran late, QA had to scramble with what little time was left over."

Anthony looks a little ticked. "We can plan out our side; we know how to set up a good QA test plan. I have done it at other companies and I try to do it here. If engineering compresses our schedule, we just do what we can to work around it. It's the nature of development. If there is a deadline, it's not like they are going to wait for QA."

Tim ponders this for a minute. "Let me walk through a few key questions and see if I can better understand and possibly help improve the situation…"

Define a Clear, Concise, and Measurable Goal

"First let's level set," Tim states. "What is the overall goal of QA?"

"To catch issues and help ensure the quality of the product," Anthony rattles off without a second thought.

"Okay, that is good on a high level, but can we be more specific?"

"Tim, do you mean our gating customer release gating criteria?" Nir sighs. "We have a whole 10-page spec if that is what you are looking for. It includes the various areas of testing, the types of testing, systems we test on, number of leads, number of hours, types and severities of issues, allowable number of issues prior to release, and so on…."

"I was more looking for a concise and measurable goal. What would the goal or mission statement be for QA on the Phoenix project?"

Anthony thinks for a second then says, "To ship a product that meets the QA customer release criteria by the November ship deadline."

"Perfect. It is *clear, measurable, and has specific criteria and dates*." Tim opens up an Excel sheet and adds the following line:

Goal: To ship a product that meets the QA customer release criteria by the November ship deadline.

List the Clear Issues and Their Impact

"So guys, what are the key issues that prevent us from meeting that goal for Phoenix?" inquires Tim.

"Everything; a ton of things based on my experience on Griffin." Nir states. "Starting with engineering. They are always late. They give us code that is not ready for testing, but if we wait for code that is stable, there would not be any time for QA. No one respects the QA process. Engineering can run as late as it wants and QA has to make up for it."

Nir and Anthony argue for 15 more minutes and then Tim steps in and summarizes their issues into an Excel spreadsheet.

Chapter 7 | Using Ambitious Targets to Handle Past Issues

Goal: To ship a product that meets the QA customer release criteria by the November ship deadline				
Issues	Raised by	Intermediate Objective IO	Owner
1. Engineering provides software that is very late and therefore limits the overall time QA has to test	Nir & Anthony		
2. Engineering software going into QA is of poor quality. For example, it crashes as soon as you start the application thus preventing any real testing.	Nir & Anthony		
3. QA is blamed for the poor software quality. We tell management that we are never given enough time, but they do not understand. They just see the poor quality and since our job is to test and validate the code then we are responsible not the engineers.	Nir & Anthony		
4. Engineering changes the requirements during development without telling QA. So when we end up testing the requirement it does not work correctly and we are unsure how to effectively test it.	Nir & Anthony		

They talked for half an hour more, but pretty much agreed that these four issues are the main ones.

Define Intermediate Objectives (IOs)

"So Tim, it is nice that we list some of the issues better, but I do not see how this solves our issues," Nir states.

"Now that we have the issues clearly defined, we need to look at each issue and see if we can come up with something to overcome it. This is known as an *intermediate objective*. By design, the person who suggested the issue gets to be the first to suggest a possible way to overcome it."

"Well, I had the first issue—*Engineering provides the software very late and therefore it limits the overall time QA has*—it seems rather pointless, because there is not much we can do to control engineering."

"So Nir, one *flying pig* suggestion is that engineering deliver code on time."

"Pretty much, Tim. It would be ideal if they were on time, but yes, based on my experience with Griffin, engineering delivering on time would be a minor miracle and an unrealistic expectation, despite what their managers and schedules claim."

"Sometime it helps to look at a wild idea and then come back and see if we can find a way to make it more realistic. For example, I'm working with the engineers on their planning. My understanding is that the Phoenix project is made up of multiple modules. So possibly we could plan to complete some of the modules earlier. It is not the same as all of the code being delivered on time, but maybe we could at least get some of it early," explains Tim.

"That would at least give us a chance to close out some of the testing on those areas and minimize the overall amount that needs to be done at the last minute," says Nir.

"It sounds promising," Anthony adds.

"It's a start, but I do not think it's nearly enough to address my concern that engineering is *always* late and in turn it reduces the time QA has to work," Nir says.

"Okay Nir, let's try it from a different angle. Let's assume that Phoenix will run badly and engineering will run late, which means QA will only have a very limited time."

"Seems more like reality than any assumption in my experience."

"So what makes sense to do in this situation, Nir?"

"Typically, our test plans go out the window. There is not enough time for a full cycle, so we just test the high risk areas the best we can."

"Since we are at the beginning of the project, is there a more methodical way we could set up up effective testing in a short time?"

"Maybe we could modularize our test plans better," Anthony indicates. "So we will have different sections of the test plan for different areas of the code. We can also set up a high-level test pass as well as a more detailed test pass. In this way, if it is a low risk area or we have tested the code before, we might be okay with a quick high-level test, and when we get to a high risk or new area, we would focus on the longer detailed pass."

"Anthony, are you sure there would be enough time for all the testing we need?" Nir inquires.

Chapter 7 | Using Ambitious Targets to Handle Past Issues

"Well, not all areas take the same amount of time, Nir. With a little bit of work, we could give an approximate amount of time it would take to do a high test pass on an area, and based on that how many overall hours we need to do a complete test cycle."

"So," Tim summarizes, "Basically, when we get down to the last few weeks, we can look at which areas we are okay doing with a high test pass and which areas we need to do a detailed test pass, add up the time it takes to run all those tests, and balance it against the time we have left."

"Pretty much," says Nir.

"Ideally, we would have the time we need, but at least this is more methodical than the two-week scrambles we've done in the past."

"So Anthony and Nir, are we comfortable that setting up a modular test plan should help us address the concern that engineering provides software late?"

"It's better than where we are at currently," Anthony chimes in a bit more enthusiastically.

"So the next issue was raised by Nir as well.—*The software going into QA is of poor quality.*"

"Yeah, this was pretty annoying. We would be delayed weeks trying to get something out of engineering to test. When we finally received something, it would just blow up as soon as we started. So we could not run any real tests, just acknowledge that it did not work. It was of little value to us and gave engineering the chance to say that had given us code to test for weeks."

"Was it all the code or just code from a few people?" Tim inquires.

"We have a few Engineers that are a little too quick to throw something that is not complete to QA. The other part is when there are tight deadlines and they are running late, the engineers are rushed and so they are quick to move code into QA."

"Nir, do you have any voice in what the engineers hand over?"

"Well Tim, one idea is that QA could refuse to test code that does not meet our quality standards."

"That sounds a little rigid Nir," states Anthony. "We want the engineers to give us early code so we can start working. The early code just needs to be something that does not just crash as soon as we try and start testing."

"Is there a test that could be done that would be a little less rigid?" inquires Tim.

Get it Done On Time!

"I guess we could set up a *simple smoke test*," states Nir. "Some basic criteria such as—the code must be able to load in the system without crashing and the features must be exercisable without immediately breaking. We are fine with early and flaky code, but it needs to have some minimal functionality."

Anthony jumps in, "We also will need to get the engineering managers to sign off on the smoke test, but it should not be too much of a problem."

"So overall, if the engineering code passes the smoke test, it can be formally accepted by QA. That sounds pretty good," Tim summarizes.

"Tim, the next issue was Anthony's—*QA is blamed for the poor software quality*. We tell management that we are never given enough time, but they do not understand."

"With the detailed high-level and detailed-level test plans, I think we can better quantify the time we need to test and the reasons for it. In the past, we just said three weeks sometimes based on a one-page plan. If we have something more comprehensive and flag what areas we are doing a high-level plan, which areas need more detailed testing, I think they will better understand the time and work involved," Anthony indicates.

"Anthony, how will you handle the last two-week mad dash? The managers state that everything is okay despite issues, then a few months later, when the customer sees the issue, they get all ticked off that QA did not catch it," Nir states, concerned.

"What if we have a formal signoff sheet? If they want us to skip certain tests, we can have them sign off on a form saying they approved it."

"So if a customer issue comes up for an area we wanted to test, we will have the documentation they signed off?"

"Pretty much. It should work. But even if they sign off on not testing something, we still should try to do some of the priority tests off the detailed test plan. Sign off or not, it is still important that we feel that a solid test has been done."

"The last one was—*Engineering changes the requirements during development without telling QA.*"

"This was a pain and just caused a lot of frustration and wasted time. Once the engineers start coding, they do not go back and update all the specs until much later. The specs are simply not their priority. We would like to talk with the engineers, but their time is pretty limited," Nir states.

"In the past, I've informally had coffee with some of the engineering managers and they often fill me in on some of the key changes. The engineers can't change something significant without their manager's approval. Maybe we just need to formalize this process. So just have a weekly update with the engineering manager on any changes not in the spec."

"Certainly worth looking into Tim. After too much pestering and the engineers having super-tight deadlines, I've had it where they would stop responding to my e-mails and calls. So if the engineering managers are more open to giving us updates on changes, it is worth a try."

"So with all of these suggestions, do you think we will be able to meet our goal? Specifically, to be able to ship a product that meets the QA customer release criteria by the November ship deadline?" Tim asks, confirming that all of the key areas have been sufficiently addressed.

"I feel better about that possibility, Tim. Much better," both Nir and Anthony indicate. Tim updates the Excel list accordingly.

Get it Done On Time!

Issues	Raised by	Intermediate Objective IO	Owner
Goal: To ship a product that meets the QA customer release criteria by the November ship deadline			
1. Engineering provides software that is very late and therefore limits the overall time QA has to test.	Nir & Anthony	a Look at ways to complete some Engineering software modules earlier.	Tim
		b Develop more detailed test plans that have high level test passes, detailed test passes, how long it takes to complete each pass, and how long it takes to complete a complete test cycle.	Anthony & Nir
2. Engineering software going into QA is of poor quality. For example, it crashes as soon as you start the application thus preventing any real testing.	Nir & Anthony	c Set up a simple smoke test that needs to be completed before checking code into QA and have the engineering managers sign off on the idea of the test.	Anthony
3. QA is blamed for the poor software quality. We tell management that we are never given enough time, but they do not understand. They just see the poor quality and since our job is to test and validate the code then we are responsible not the engineers.	Nir & Anthony	d Use the more detailed test plans to better quantify to management the time needed for testing.	Anthony
		e Set up a formal sign-off sheet to document testing that management wants to skip tests due to time constraints.	Anthony
4. Engineering changes the requirements during development without telling QA. So when we end up testing the requirement it does not work correctly and we are unsure how to effectively test it.	Nir & Anthony	f Work to set up a weekly meeting with engineering managers to review code changes not captured in the spec.	Tim, Anthony

Sequence the Intermediate Objectives (IOs)

Tim looks at Nir and Anthony, "So based on our discussions, I captured and labeled the following suggestions:

- A. Look at ways to complete some of the engineering software modules earlier.
- B. Develop more detailed test plans that have high-level test passes, detailed test passes, how long it takes to complete each pass, and how long it takes to complete a complete test cycle.

- C. Set up a simple smoke test that needs to be completed before checking code into QA and have the engineering managers sign off on the idea of the test.
- D. Use the more detailed test plans to better quantify to management the time needed for testing.
- E. Set up a formal signoff sheet to document testing that management wants to skip tests due to time constraints.
- F. Work to set up a weekly meeting with engineering managers to review code changes not captured in the spec.

It is not too bad of a list, but we cannot do all of them at once. We should go through and see which ones make sense to do first. It would also be good to *specify an owner and a timeline for each suggestion* as well. Anthony, based on the list, would [A] look at ways to complete some engineering software modules earlier come before [B] develop more detailed test plans?"

Anthony indicates, "They both can pretty much be done in parallel."

"I can follow up on looking at ways to complete software modules early over the next few weeks since I am meeting with the engineers," Tim suggests.

"Nir and I can work on the test plans. It will take us about a month, but we are pretty early in the test process, so there is time."

"Okay, Anthony, so for [C] set up the smoke test, would it come before [A] complete some modules early or [B] develop more detailed test plans, or would they be done in parallel?" asks Tim.

"Again something in parallel. I can look at it over the next week or so. Given that I was burned by it pretty bad on Griffin, I have a pretty clear idea of what we need. Once it is done, Nir and I can meet with the engineering managers."

"Sounds good. So would [D] use the test plans to better quantify to management the time needed to do testing go after [B] develop more detailed test plans?" asks Tim.

"We need the plans first, and then we can use them to help level set management on how long it takes to test. Once we are pretty comfortable with the test, I can bring it up with the regular bi-weekly meeting I have with some of the management team. After that I can look at bringing it in for a formal manager review," Anthony explains.

"Okay Anthony, looking at the Excel sheet, this is what I have so far for our plan. A, B, and C can be done in parallel. D can be done only once we have completed B."

Get it Done On Time!

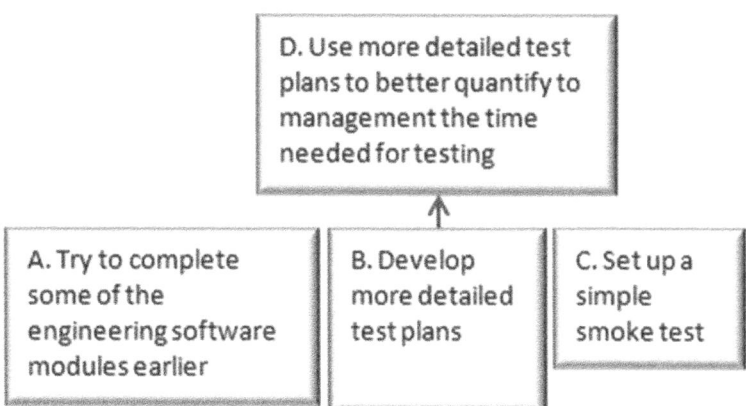

"What about [E] set up a formal sign-up sheet when management wants to skip tests due to time constraints?" inquires Tim.

"That one is a little touchy," Nir says, jumping in. "Definitely after [B] set up the test plans, probably better after [D] get management to see how long the test plans are and what they involve. I can set up the basic form. Anthony, since you are working with the managers, can you take this one?"

"That is fine," states Anthony. "I will bring it up as we do the manager review of the test plans. If they know they might be asked to sign off on something, they will be a lot more attentive about what the test plan says."

"The last one—[F] work to set up a weekly meeting with the engineering manager to review code changes?" Tim continues.

"I can take that one," Anthony volunteers, "Since I already talk with the engineering manager. I can meet with him over the next month or so. In regards to your question, we should be able to do that in parallel with the other tasks."

"So, looking at the Excel sheet, this is what I have for our plan," Tim explains.

Chapter 7 | Using Ambitious Targets to Handle Past Issues

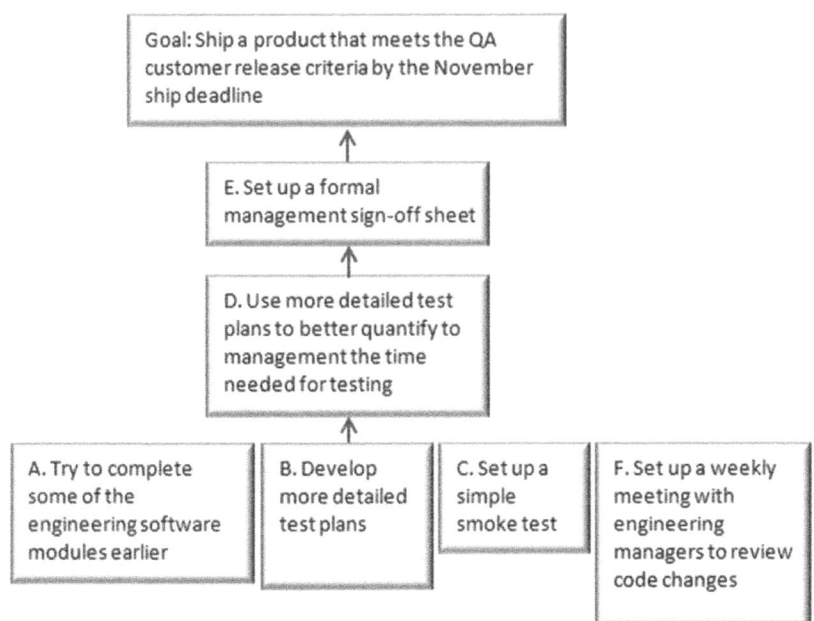

"Looks like a good start, Tim. What if we find additional items later on?" inquires Nir.

"Duh," states Anthony, "We just add them to the plan."

"Correct Anthony," confirms Tim, "We can continue to build out the plan as needed. We do not want to get too detailed, but we do need to cover the key areas."

Results

"So Nir and Anthony, before we wrap up this meeting, what do you think about the process we went through and the plan we developed?," asks Tim.

"Well Tim, to be honest, based on Griffin, I was feeling pretty burned out and seeing the whole test process as pointless," states Nir. "Sure, the test plans helped in the beginning, but at the end we just had to wing it. I was sure Phoenix was just going to be another repeat of Griffin. Going through this exercise, I feel a bit more optimistic and empowered. There will be issues, but at least I feel like there is something we can do to try ahead of time to improve the situation."

"Actually Tim, I like the fact that you could take Nir's endless complaining and put it to good use," states Anthony. "All kidding aside, you let him vent his issues and once we were done with that, we turned around and started to constructively look at what we could do to address the issues he had raised."

"The part I liked Tim is that you did not just complain or dictate a plan. Anthony and I were involved and able to share our different concerns and insights. Overall, we provided the detail and helped to put the plan together. We have ownership of it."

"I'm glad I could help," states Tim. "Now I need to catch up with Gary and see how he is doing."

FRT

Just as Tim leaves, he pulls out his FRT diagram and adds one more box: 13) we improve our quality assurance testing.

Chapter 7 | Using Ambitious Targets to Handle Past Issues

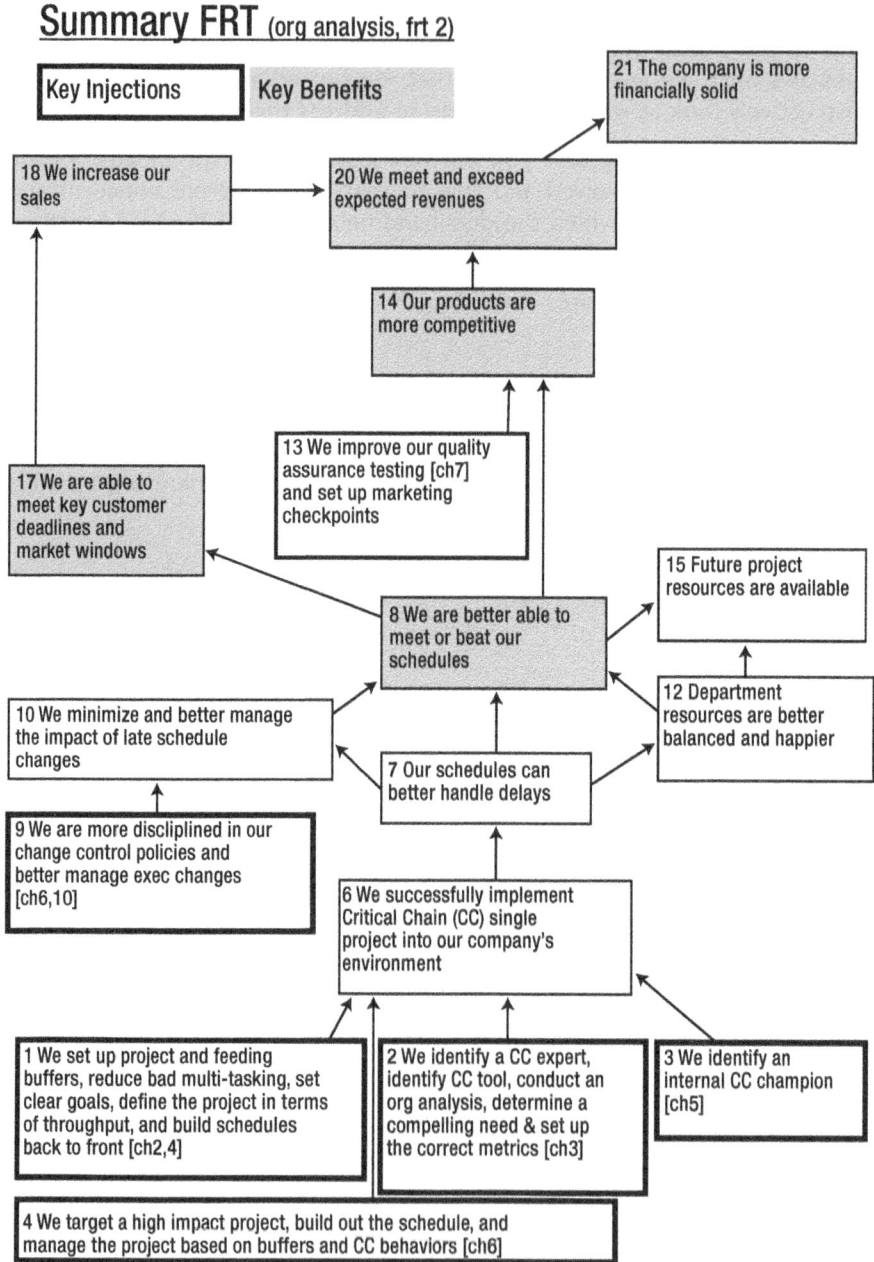

CHAPTER 8

Individual Buy-In

Tim, Randal, and Gary quickly grab some coffee and head off to a small conference room.

"So Tim, the Exec review is coming up in a few weeks," states Randal. "We need to be ready for it. Micky is going to overview the direction of the company and we need to be able to show that we can support that vision. Gary, how are we doing with the results?"

"I am gathering them up now. We are already seeing benefits just with the schedule build and Critical Chain process for Phoenix. Give it a few more weeks and we can see how well the schedule is holding up in execution and how well we hit our first milestone."

"Sounds good. Gary, I can work with you to put the slides for the Exec review together. How about you, Tim? Where are you at with meeting with the execs?"

Tim pauses briefly, not used to seeing Randal in a take-charge mode before. "I need to meet with Ashley in sales and marketing and Herb in HR so I can capture their key issues. From there, I can complete the overall organizational analysis. I also have a meeting scheduled with Grant the COO and Micky. I wanted to check what their concerns are as well, but more importantly get their buy-in on the direction we are going with implementing Critical Chain."

Randal looks at Tim for a bit and takes a deep breath, "Grant and Micky are both on board so both of them are key players. And with the Exec review coming up, Micky has been on a bit of a war path lately. He's been super busy and super touchy. Most of us have been giving him more space than usual."

"I can tell from the Griffin project post-mortem. I'll be careful," responds Tim.

© Eric Bergland 2016
E. Bergland, *Get it Done On Time!*, DOI 10.1007/978-1-4842-1860-0_8

Chapter 8 | Individual Buy-In

"Actually Tim it would be good for me to sit in on your meeting with Grant so I can see what you present and if there are key items I could pull into the overall Exec presentation."

"Sure Randal, I think that would be a great idea. How much does Grant know about Critical Chain?"

"He has shown a good amount of interest in the Critical Chain concepts I have shared with him in the one-on-one meetings we've had. I mainly covered the high-level concepts, but he seems to get it and asks a good number of questions. What is your take, Gary?"

"I agree," says Gary, "Grant has an engineering background and is more hands on. He wants to know the details of what is going on. He has already agreed with applying Critical Chain to the Phoenix project and we've spent a few meetings going into the implementation details and how it is different than what we did on the Griffin project."

"That sounds very promising. Randal, does Micky, Ashley, or Herb have any background on Critical Chain?"

"Not really, Tim. I have talked with Micky and he has listened. But Ashley and Herb generally do not get too involved in the particulars of how engineering operates. They usually defer to Gary, Grant, and Micky unless there is some impact to their area."

"Okay, good to know. Randal, I have a meeting with Ashley and Herb later today. Once I have done that can we possibly sync up before the meeting with Grant and Micky and strategize?"

"Sure, Tim."

Meeting with the Sales and Marketing Director

Over the next few days, Tim follows up with some of the execs in prep for the upcoming Exec review. The first person Tim decides to follow up with is Ashley, the interim sales and marketing director covering for Micky. Tim takes the elevator to the executive floor and walks down the well carpeted hall to her office. Tim then carefully knocks on the door.

"Hey Tim, you are right on time. Come on in." Tim slowly walks into her office. It has a huge window overseeing the company campus. In front of it is a very classic solid wood desk with a few chairs in front of it.

"Tim, feel free to sit down. I have just a few minutes and then I have my next meeting," says Ashley.

Get it Done On Time!

Ashley is a tall blonde who is probably in her mid 40s. She wears a cream colored business-like skirt and jacket. "Sure," replies Tim, "Thank you for fitting me into your schedule."

"So Tim, I'm short on time. Is there something specific you want to discuss and I can try and help you the best I can."

"Sure, I'm working with Gary and Randal to improve the company's project management and engineering. But I am also seeing that a lot of the issues are crossing departments and holding back the company as a whole. I wanted to know from your side what key issues you were seeing in your area."

"Why?"

"I believe that if we can help engineering it will not only help them, but help the company overall."

"Kinda, if they succeed we all will exceed?" Asks Ashley.

"Yes."

"Fair enough," Ashley replies matter of factly. Pausing for a moment and thinking things over, she continues, "Like you said, the engineering issues are not just confined to engineering. Engineering has been regularly missing deadlines. The customer contracts we set up require key features to be delivered by set time frames. We regularly miss those dates and drop the features [crt 20]. This incurs penalties. Worse, we get less desirable terms the next time around or lose future contracts altogether [crt 25]. Micky has even been making regular calls, both within the United States and internationally to see what possibilities there are. But overall, we are not meeting our revenue targets [crt 26] and have to change something. But you should be aware of that already."

"True," states Tim. "So if we improved our ability to deliver, it would dramatically improve things?"

"Yes, once we can prove it was not a one-time success, we can work on repairing our damaged and strained customer relationships [crt 27]. Micky has been doing a tremendous job trying to keep them happy and not to drop our contracts. But he can only do so much. But honestly, between Micky and I and some of the other execs engineering has very much lost our trust. We do not see how they are going to improve. Micky once asked me to look into adding more product lines [crt 30], figuring if we made less per product we could try and make it up with more products."

"This would make engineering's work load even worse. It would cripple them," says Tim, very concerned.

"Agreed. We considered it, saw how many additional lines we would need, and then dropped it. We didn't think engineering could deliver. And there is more."

"More?" Tim inquires.

"Our competitors are building up their resources and expertise; they are getting several of the contracts we once had. Their quality is going up; they are getting more efficient and more experienced [crt 22]. If we do not move faster, they *will* catch up and surpass us." Ashley says in a very serious tone. "Micky is working on a way out of it and he is pretty furious at engineering for putting him and the company in this spot."

"I understand. We have made great progress with engineering, Ashley. The development process is running better. We are on track to meet our milestones. Gary is pulling together the latest data now."

"We have heard that claim from engineering before."

"I understand. We are gathering the data to back up the claims and we are getting the schedules back in line. That will enable us to be on time and feature complete as well as enable us to do more R&D. That would make the products more competitive. That should help you improve the customer relationships [frt 19]."

"And if engineering sacrifices quality to hit schedules again?"

"We can add marketing checkpoints [frt 13] along the development process to review the feature development and ensure it is in sync with customer and contract needs as long as it is part of a change control process," Tim explains.

Ashley looks down at her calendar. "It sounds promising Tim, but it really depends on Micky. My 3 PM meeting is just starting up. If you can excuse me, I need to call in. Possibly we can talk more after the board meeting and see."

"Okay, thank you for your time." Tim states as he walks out of Ashley's office and closes the door. He hopes that the results and progress he has made with Gary and Randal are enough to show that things are turning around. At the same time, he is wondering if Ashley was holding back.

Meeting with Human Resources (HR)

Tim wanders down a floor to the HR department. As he approaches Herb's door, he hears him on the phone chatting and joking. Tim lightly knocks on the door. Herb looks up and over his reading glasses.

"Hey, come on in Tim. I'm glad to catch up with you again."

Get it Done On Time!

Herb is average height, filled out with a bit of a belly and dressed in khaki pants, an untucked dress shirt, a vest, and comfortable dress shoes. "Sure Herb," Tim responds, "I'm not interrupting?"

"No, never." He tells the person on the other line he has a meeting and will catch him later in the day. "So Tim, sorry about the delays getting your desk and phone. With the new hires, a few people leaving, and moving things around, it's been a bit chaotic."

"No problem, Herb. As I noted in my e-mail I just wanted to follow up on a few things. I have been working with Gary and Randal to improve our project management and help engineering. I'm feeling several of the issues they are running into are not limited to engineering. Are there other issues you see holding back the company?"

"Sure Tim, I can help. Is this just for you or something else?"

"I'm talking with other managers and looking to see what their top-level issues are and trying to see how they interconnect. So I will just share the top-level issues not the details of the conversations."

"And the audience is..."

"Exec staff," said Tim.

"Fair enough. Just needed to know my audience. So I'm sure you have been seeing the various going-away lunch invites. We're losing good people [crt 14]. Some due to jitters about how we are doing, others just burning out. Worse, some of our *competitors* are ramping up and have picked up some of our people and those people in turn have lead our competitors to try and poach other people from our company. It's a bit disheartening."

"The high pressure to deliver was driving them away?"

"Tight deadlines, priorities switching, unrealistic schedules, and adding more work to already unrealistic deadlines have been most of the complaints I've heard during the exit interviews. I have heard from a few people that Phoenix is looking better thanks to your help. But yes, people are stressing out and burning out. Micky stepping up things added more pressure."

"Fair enough, Herb. Like you said, we are making great progress with Phoenix and we are getting back on track."

"That is great to hear, Tim. It is nice to have some good news again. Things are still tight. I am hoping your changes are going to stick. One of the past items out of Micky's Exec meetings that concerned me a great deal was his discussion to see if we could stem the corporate revenue bleeding by cutting 10% of the resources across the company [crt 29]."

"That is pretty drastic."

Chapter 8 | Individual Buy-In

"Things are tight and have gotten worse over the last few months, Tim. The various managers have already had to identify the resources for the 10% reduction and at the same time promise to maintain existing commitments."

"Will Micky go through with the reduction?" Tim asks, concerned.

"Unsure. I figure it might come up in the Exec review. But Micky knows that it would be a short-term fix and in the long run likely do more damage than good. My guess is that it was a bit of a scare tactic to shake things up and get the managers to move and see how dire things are. I figured you should know, but please do not pass this info around. People are already jittery. Like I said, it's good to hear you are making progress. Hopefully they can step it up and the company can focus on moving ahead."

"Definitely. Gary has some encouraging results he will be reviewing in the Exec review. We are making great progress. As we get the schedules running better it should dramatically reduce the priority thrashing and unrealistic deadlines, and better manage the new requests, which will enable people to better focus and not burn out [frt 12]."

"Great to hear, Tim. If you need anything from my side, my door is always open."

"Thank you for the support, Herb."

Randal and Tim Prep for the Meeting with Grant

Randal strides into Tim's new cube. "So Tim, all settled in?" He looks around and sees the three blank gray walls of Tim's cube—no pictures, no papers, just a laptop, computer bag, table, and a chair.

"Pretty much, Randal. It just became official a few days ago. It's not much, but it works."

"So how did the meetings with Herb and Ashley go?"

"Pretty well, Randal. I picked up a few more details that are helping me get a more complete overall picture."

"Good to hear." Randal says, a bit anxious. "So Tim for the Exec meeting coming up it will be just a small group of key people focusing on Gary and Micky's updates. Me, you, and Gary can present the engineering update. Gary owns the overall update, but he often lets me cover a few slides that tie in engineering and marketing. You can cover any Critical Chain detailed questions that come up. As interim CEO, Micky will provide the update on the company strategy. The board itself has three members. Other than that there will be Herb and Ashley."

"Who are the decision makers?" inquires Tim.

"Micky, Grant, and the external board members."

"Hmm, I have meetings with Grant and Micky to talk with them before the Exec meeting. Do the external board members have any Critical Chain experience?" Asks Tim.

"Unlikely Tim. Mainly they will defer to Gary or Grant for the engineering details, then see how Micky weighs in. If everything falls in line, things will go forward. If there are disagreements then the whole board will step in, review the issues, and provide some directives that it will expect to be carried out. So we have some time, but not much. What is your plan to talk with Grant?"

"Mainly I need to get his buy-in. Not just to Critical Chain, but how everything is tied together and impacts the whole company."

"Tim, you have just an hour with Grant and his schedule is pretty packed. You're not going to try and fit in the whole high-level Critical Chain concepts, what is needed to implement, and we need a champion with him are you?" Randal asks, a bit nervous.

"No no. More succinct and high level. We have two phases. The first is the behind-the-scenes homework where we leverage our organizational analysis and work through the six layers of resistance. The second phase is the actual presentation to the customer where we conversationally pull key items from the work we did for the six layers."

"So the six layers is like a 12-step program?" Asks Randal.

Tim sighs, "To buy in to a new concept such as the Theory of Constraints or Critical Chain, we organize our analysis into the six layers of resistance. This way we can step through our buy-in proposal in an effective and systematic way, help address people's concerns, and help them understand and ideally agree to our proposal."

Randal looks at Tim oddly.

"Here, let me walk you through the layers:

- Layer 1: Lack of consensus on the problem
- Layer 2: We do not agree on the direction of the solution
- Layer 3: Arguing the proposed solution cannot yield the desired outcome
- Layer 4: Yes, *but*. Concerns about potential side-effects from the proposed solution
- Layer 5: Obstacles that stand in the way of implementing the solution into the environment
- Layer 6: Raising doubts, wait and see, unverbalized fears"

"Tim, why are you always so cryptic. You have a sales process. I've seen similar things before. Build rapport, learn something about the customer, understand their issues, etc.."

"Kinda. It certainly has parallels to a sales process, but also specific tie-ins to the Theory of Constraints tools. For example, 'layer 1: lack of consensus' is based on the CRT we have been working on." Tim takes out the CRT diagram and shares it with Randal.

"Whoa! Tim that diagram is pretty complex. I have watched you build it. But someone seeing it as a whole, especially for the first time, can be pretty overwhelming."

"The key part is that it captures all of the different issues, ties them together, and helps us focus on the organization's core conflict and root causes of our problems."

"Okay Tim, I can certainly agree that the CRT is capturing our issues, but please tell me you were not planning to share that with Grant or at least not on your first meeting with him?"

"It's tempting…" Tim admits.

Randal looks harshly at Tim.

"It's tempting since it took a good amount of work to create and it does a really, really good job of summarizing the issues and their interconnections, but like you said it's a bit overwhelming especially if you are not familiar with TOC," concedes Tim.

"That sounds much better Tim," Randal says, breathing a sigh of relief, "So what is your real plan?"

"Similar to the conversation we had when we first talked about your company [Chapter 2]. I'll pull out a few of the major issues that impact the company and are likely to resonate with Grant. From there, we can quantify how significant they are and confirm that he agrees that they are inter-related. Likely he knows how they inter-relate, but if not I have the CRT I can fall back on and conversationally walk him through. That should cover layer 1, which is to agree on the problem."

"Hmm, Tim, couldn't you have simply said you need to identify and quantify the customer's biggest pain points and loosely show they're inter-related? It sounds so much simpler."

"Possibly. I guess. One other key item with the CRT and meeting with Grant. We need to be sure to blame the system. It is not that any one person or group is trying to undermine the company. The system, the way we operate, is holding us back. The CRT outlines this system and how it is interconnected. We need to focus our efforts on understanding, blaming, and changing the system."

Get it Done On Time!

"Interesting approach. So the system is the fall guy and the one we go after."

"It avoids finger pointing and helps us move forward in a productive and problem solving way," explains Tim.

"I'm curious to see this in action. So what's next?"

"I talk about the struggle (conflict) that the company is in, how it really challenges us, and how it drives the major issues."

"Why bother, Tim?"

"We want to focus Grant's attention to one central and critical struggle. From there, we can propose our solution (layer 2) and then immediately start dealing with the next question, which is why do you feel this solution will address the problems (layer 3)."

"Hmm. It feels like you are taking all of the key pain points and pulling them all together into one single overall pain point/organizational struggle."

"Focusing our efforts, yes. The main part is that we want to focus on the system and the challenges to the system, not any one specific department or person."

"So Tim, how are you going to sell the fact that your solution is the one that will work and is better than other competing ideas, solutions, or products? As we say in sales, why should I buy this from you?"

"I have my FRT." Tim then takes out his FRT diagram and shows it to Randal.

Randal rolls his eyes. "Tim, *not* another overly complicated diagram."

"As before, it would be fun to show Grant all the hard work that went into creating this and how wonderful it is. Unfortunately when you start showing CRTs, FRTs, and start using TOC lingo to people who are not familiar with TOC—instead of them being amazed by your insights—they in fact get turned off by the complexity and your arrogance in assuming they would understand something so new and different instantly. As you note, I will conversationally pick out a few key items, quantify them, and do my best to translate them into terms that are familiar to the organization and to that individual."

"Sounds promising, again translating back into English, focus on the key benefits and value to the organization. I have seen you build out the FRT. It makes sense to me on a high level, but it's not something someone would just understand right away. So Tim, after you *conversationally* share your grand vision and Grant is stunned with your brilliance, what happens next? Are we done?"

"For this meeting, yes. If we can agree on the problem (layer 1), direction of the solution (layer 2), and that Critical Chain will get us to where we need to be (layer 3), we should be good! If Grant has additional questions we can certainly address them as they come up. This is also covered by the six layers.

Chapter 8 | Individual Buy-In

Layer 4 is yes, *but* (fear of some negative consequence), Layer 5 is you can't because (some obstacle blocks us), and Layer 6 is hesitation to move forward even after all concerns have been addressed. We can proactively think of likely concerns and responses. But for this meeting, we should just focus on any specific questions he has. As you say, keep it simple."

Randal shakes his head back and forth, "Well Tim, as usual you are very through if not a bit overwhelming. Your sales model seems pretty complete. Just one last item. Where do you seal the deal?"

"Actually that is the last critical piece. Closing the deal. We are meeting with Grant for a reason. We should be sure we get Grant's commitment to take some action, otherwise why have this meeting in the first place."

"With the company running out of time and the Exec meeting coming up, we want Grant on our side. We need him to help promote and back up our recommendation," restates Randal.

"Exactly."

"Actually Tim, one more thing. Stepping back—why bother? I mean why bother with the organizational analysis, CRT, FRT, getting all of the execs to buy-in? Wouldn't it just be simpler to just build the Critical Chain schedules, add the buffers, and implement it in engineering without the rest of the organization's involvement?"

"It could work, but briefly. In the long run it would likely fall apart. As I noted in the factors for success [Chapter 3], the organizational buy-in is needed. If management is not on board and they see the project buffers, they will just cut them and that will undermine Critical Chain's success. With the cut project buffers we are more likely to miss deadlines and in turn management will push even more to switch to some other methodology du jour. The same is true with the buffer management and project behaviors. Without management support they will not work and in turn the Critical Chain solution will not work."

"So what if we got Gary and Grant behind it and told the others to let engineering manage the schedules the way they need to without interference?"

"It's a team sport. We're trying to improve the whole company. The whole system, not just one department. Think of it like a rowing boat. If everyone is in sync, we will move forward and quickly. If someone moves too slow or even too fast the whole boat goes off course. Just look at where things are at now. Engineering is struggling and Micky is just adding more changes and more work. They're not in sync."

Sighing, Randal concedes, "I guess you're right, Tim. Ideally we need to get everyone working together. Engineering is just where we are seeing all of the issues."

"Yep, speaking of getting everyone to work together, it's time to meet with Grant."

"Tim Tim Tim—the things you are getting me into…"

"I'm helping to build your character."

"Ahh Tim…so many things I could say to that," Randle chuckles.

Meeting with Grant

Tim and Randal head up to exec row and over to Grant's office. Like Ashley's office, it is well appointed with filled book cases and a solid wood desk, and then it differs from there. Grant's desk is covered with piles of paper. What does not fit on the desk overflows to the nearby chairs. Grant is easily in his 50s with black and gray peppered hair. He is dressed in a very sharp business suit and carries himself with an athletic stride.

"Hi Tim," Grant walks up to the door to greet him. "I have been interested in meeting you."

"Hi Grant, thank you for making the time to meet with me."

"Hi Randal, please come in as well."

"So Tim," Grant starts, "I appreciate the time and effort you have been putting in working with Gary and Randal. Given the Griffin issues, your timing is pretty good."

"Thank you, it's a good group of people."

"So Tim you called the meeting. What can I do for you?"

"With the Exec meeting coming up in a few weeks I wanted to talk to you about the Critical Chain work we've been doing and how it can have an overall impact on the company."

"Fair enough, Tim. Gary and Randal have been keeping me up to date on the consulting work you have been doing as far as ramping them up on the Critical Chain methodology as well as the Phoenix schedule build. They have been very positive about it. So I was assuming this was something engineering and project focused."

"Critical Chain and TOC will certainly help engineering, but it can have a much broader impact than that. And we *need* that broader impact to help the company succeed and grow.

"How so," Grant asks, curious to see where Tim is going with this.

Quantifying the Issues

"When I first started, the key issue was that we were slipping schedules more and more [crt 15]. The prior product development system was very aggressive and did not handle delays well. We were struggling to meet our existing requests and, even worse, the new requests we are making."

"Correct Tim, that was one of the reasons Gary and I were interested in seeing how you could help us."

"And to just put some numbers around this about this, I'm guessing about 40-60% of the schedules were late by some amount?"

"Worse now than before, but about 40%. Some a few days late and the ones that really blew out were a month or more. Gary and I had put various initiatives in place to try and tighten things up. Some of these initiatives worked, but others not as well as we hoped." Grant explains.

"And this impacted the perception of how well the engineering department was operating?" Asks Tim.

"Very much so. It's something that concerns Gary and me a great deal. We even tried juggling our project priorities between proprietary features and infrastructure versus general features and infrastructure but it all needs to be done [crt 12b]."

"And the prior scheduling system's slipped schedules would in-turn impact customer deadlines [crt 25] and customer relationships [crt 27]. This would then impact the company's existing and future contracts, putting more pressure on the company?"

"Yes, Tim."

"Is it possible to quantify how contracts have been impacted?"

"Marketing and sales could probably give you some numbers. It's a bit intangible since there are a variety of factors that impact if we win or lose a contract, but I've heard Micky state the revenues from contracts are down 30% and putting a great amount of financial pressure on the company [crt 28]. Thus his ambitious charter to reverse the decline and grow the company by 20%."

Explaining the Core Conflict and Key Injection

"So stepping back a bit, the company is under great pressure. Our current project management system is failing us. On the one side, we want and struggle to meet existing contracts. At the same time we find that we must work to grow the company to make up for lost revenues. We do not have the resources to do both, but we find ourselves struggling to trying to do one, the other, or both. In the meantime our schedules slip, our customers get upset, our revenues decline, and the company's financial situation gets worse."

Grant pauses a bit and ponders for a moment and takes a deep breath. "That is quite a statement, Tim. So I agree that our current project management system has its shortcomings and we're having some significant problems, but what would you recommend?"

"I strongly suggest that we need to put Critical Chain into place with a few key additional items."

"That is a bit much to take on faith, Tim. Can you elaborate?"

Walking Through the Vision/FRT

"Sure. So there are a few key reasons why Critical Chain would help us address the various issues the company is facing:

- Build out the schedule to the point we generate revenue (throughput [frt 1])
- Protect the deadline and behaviors (project buffers [frt 1])
- Look at the whole organization (organizational analysis [frt 2])"

Walking Through the Vision: Throughput

"Okay, Tim."

"One key part is that traditionally your schedules are often built to the point that it is engineering complete. But that is not the point we generate revenue. The customer still has to integrate and confirm the feature is functional per the contract. Randal, my understanding is that this can sometimes take about a month?"

"Give or take. It depends on how complicated the features are and how ready the customer is to integrate it. It go a bit longer if additional back-and-forth discussions are required"

"So with the Phoenix schedule we are building in sync points with the customer and aligning our resources to better help them integrate and confirm faster. This adds a bit more to the schedule, but overall it helps us generate revenue from the project much faster."

"It's an interesting idea, Tim. Gary said something similar and that with Phoenix he figures the customers will feel we are better engaged and it should go much faster."

Walking Through the Vision: Project Buffers and Behaviors

"The next part is that we are working to better use the time available in the project. As with any project *variability* is critical. At any time tasks can take longer than expected—surprises, issues, and problems all happen. It is the very nature of projects. The tricky part is that once delays start to accumulate people can only react by compromising the project. They cut scope, add resources and spend more, or push out deadlines. Critical Chain challenges this."

"How?"

"With Critical Chain, we create a bank of time. Any time there is a delay we can take time out of this bank versus having to cut scope, add resources and go over budget, or push out due date," Tim explains.

"We don't want to add more time to the schedule. Where does this time come from?"

Tim continues, "So let me give you an example. If I asked my son to give me a very conservative estimate on how long it would take to mow the lawn, he might say an hour. And if he did it very quickly with no issues he would say the focused time would be 35 minutes. So I manage the task to the 35-minute focused time and put the remaining 25 minutes (60-35=25) into a bank. If it takes him 45 minutes then I use up the 35 minutes of focused time and use 10 minutes from the bank of time. But it also leaves me with 15 minutes left over in the bank. I can use this remaining time to cover any delays from any other tasks he was working on."

"Okay Tim, I think I understand what you are trying to say on a high level. You subtract the focused times from the overall estimates and use that to create a bank of time. Then you drive people to the focused times. Any time there is a delay, you take the time out of the bank. It kinda makes sense, but I would feel better seeing a real example."

"Sure. Gary and I can walk you through the Phoenix schedule and you can see the focused times we're driving the team to, the overall estimates, and the bank of time we have setup. You can also ask Gary how much of the project we have completed compared to how much of the bank of time we have used."

"Okay Tim, I'll ask him in our one-on-one next week."

Walking Through the Vision: Organizational Analysis

"The next part is that we are not blindly putting the Critical Chain methodology into your environment and expecting it to magically fix everything. I have gone through and reviewed the organization to better understand the challenges and overall issues. As I noted, the current project-management process is not working. Building the schedules to revenue can help us move faster. Setting up the bank of time can help us protect our deadlines. This helps us with our original commitments."

"Okay Tim."

"But there is also the challenge and need of growing the business at the same time. For example, there are urgent customer requests, exec reviews, adding new projects, and the quality assurance (QA) process. The bank of time (project buffers) can help with this some, but it can't absorb all of it. That is where additional key items are needed. On the QA side I worked with Nir and Anthony to create a better and more flexible process [frt 13]. If we know that we can expect customer requests and exec review changes, we can reserve some capacity for these items, but we really need a more disciplined change control process. Regardless of how well we design our system, if we flood it with work it will eventually fail."

"I have talked with Micky in the past about this. He has expressed two main concerns. We *have* to grow the business and engineering needs to move faster," presses Grant.

"We can show how we can help grow the business. With the Phoenix project, we can show that we can move faster and more reliably. With the reserved capacity we can accommodate some urgent customer requests and exec changes. We can provide more consistent and on-time delivery to customers, which will improve our relationships and future contracts. But we will lose this and put the company at risk if we don't have effective change control."

"Tim, I can talk with Micky and the board about this. I like the way you framed it. We don't need change control to limit our growth, we need it to *enable* our growth. I think that will better resonate with the team and move us forward, as opposed to them thinking that engineering is just complaining again," Grant says excitedly.

Walking Through the Vision: Summary

"So lastly is the old versus the new," Tim continues, "With the old scheduling system we could not consistently meet our original commitments. In addition, we could not do the things we needed to grow the company. Departments were getting stretched out. Schedules were slipping. We missed key deadlines and damaged our customer relationships."

"Okay," acknowledges Grant.

"With the new process we have added a bank of time (project buffer), built the schedules to capture revenues quicker, added capacity to accommodate growth requests, and improved quality assurance and change control. This sets us up to be successful and in turn reliably deliver features to our customers, improve our relationships and grow our business with them, which increases our revenues."

Close the Deal

"You make a very compelling argument, Tim. It sound much more promising. Let me review some of these items with Gary and we will need to see how well Phoenix does."

"That is great to hear, Grant."

Randal then gently slaps Tim on the shoulder. "*Close the deal.*"

"Of course, go ahead," Tim pushes back.

"Ug," Randal turns to Grant, "So Grant, based on what you have seen, can you back us up in the Exec meeting?"

Grant puts his hand on his chin and ponders for a moment. "I was going to wait and see what Micky was proposing. Likely more marketing plans and strategies. He has been working hard on something."

"A lot is at risk and we're running out of time," Randal presses.

"Fair enough, Randal. There are a few weeks until the Exec review. I want to see if Phoenix stays on track and review your plan with Gary. A lot rides on his team's ability to put Critical Chain into place and get results from it. If he's confident, then I can back you up."

"Sounds good. Thanks Grant." Randal replies.

Final Current Reality Tree

After the meeting, Tim sits down with Randal.

"So Randal, are you ready for the final tweaks to the CRT?"

"Sure Tim. It looks like you have grown it quite a bit."

Get it Done On Time!

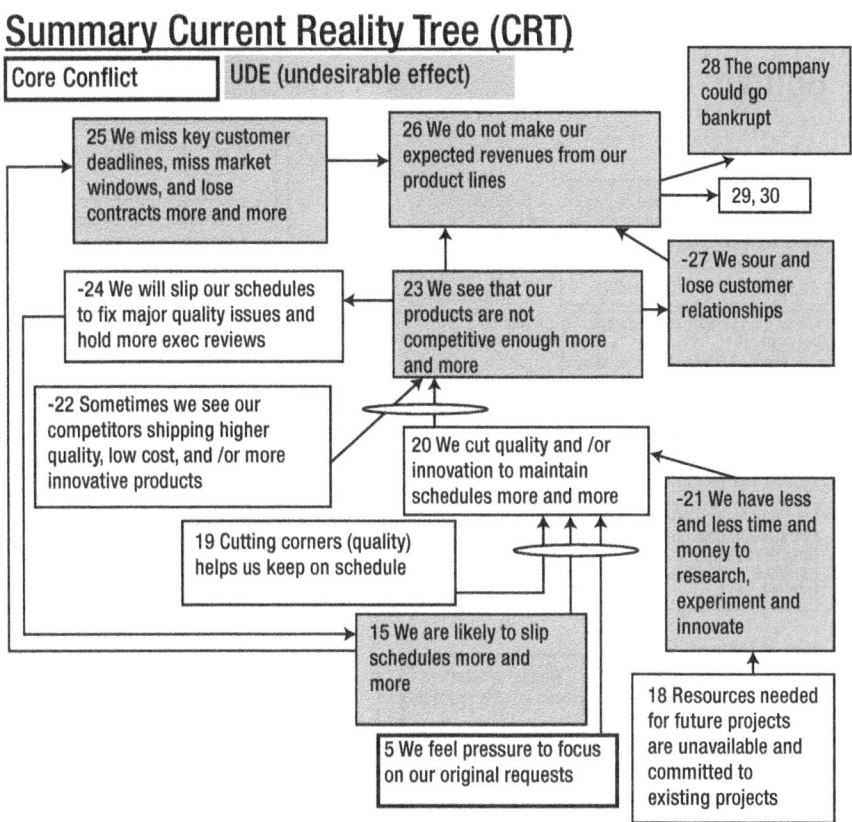

"So I split the CRT to top and bottom since it was getting too big to fit on one page. Not ideal, but it works. On the top of the tree, we can see higher-level management issues. After meeting with Ashley I wanted to add and clarify two items. 22) We see that are competitors are catching up, specifically their quality is going up, their features are improving, and their costs are going down. The second was 27) we sour and lose customer relationships."

"Makes sense Tim. Competition and customer relationships are two of her major concerns."

"I also added two clarifications. First, 23) if our products are not competitive then 24) we will slip schedules and hold additional Exec reviews. Lastly, 21) we have less time to research is one of the consequences from 18) resources for future projects are unavailable."

"Ug Tim, you are capturing even more complications." Randal admits.

"Just trying to capture all of the major issues. Next is the bottom of the CRT. This is where the drivers of the higher-level management issues appear."

Chapter 8 | Individual Buy-In

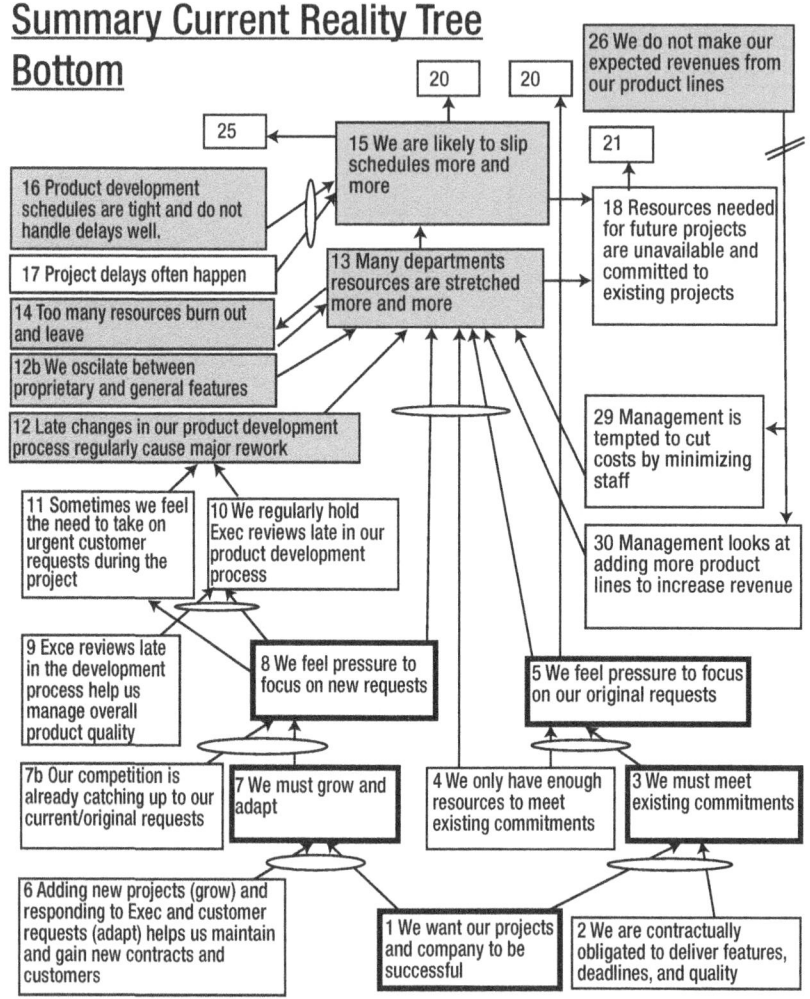

"So Randal, based on our conservation with Grant I added that 12b) we oscillate between proprietary and generic features. In talking with Ashley and Herb, I am adding 30) management looks at adding more projects and 29) management is tempted to cut costs by minimizing staff."

"Minimizing staff?"

"Management is under pressure. If we can't make enough revenue from existing products there are two ways you can go. Add more products or reduce staff. Management has looked at both, but neither is viable."

"A bit scary Tim, but yes. We have enough trouble with our existing products to try and add more. And we're busy with existing products, so cutting staff will just put us farther behind. Just looking at *all* the issues you have captured on both pages makes me feel a bit more depressed about your doom tree."

"Well, the goal of the CRT is not to depress everyone. The goal is to show the connections between the issues, see where to focus efforts, and show the compelling need to change."

"Well Tim, we all knew we needed to change. This just is showing us how much has to change. It is looking like everything."

"But the key is that everything is connected. We need to focus on the conflict between original requests and new requests and we need to look at what is going into 13) departments are stretched."

"Well Tim, I knew engineering is a target, but in looking at 13) I can see eight arrows going into it. That is a target if I ever saw one."

"We need to fix the system, not a specific issue or department. If we focus on the drivers (bottom of the tree) the changes should carry up through the tree with the help of a few key injections. Here, let's walk through the FRT. It should be much more encouraging."

Chapter 8 | Individual Buy-In

Future Reality Tree

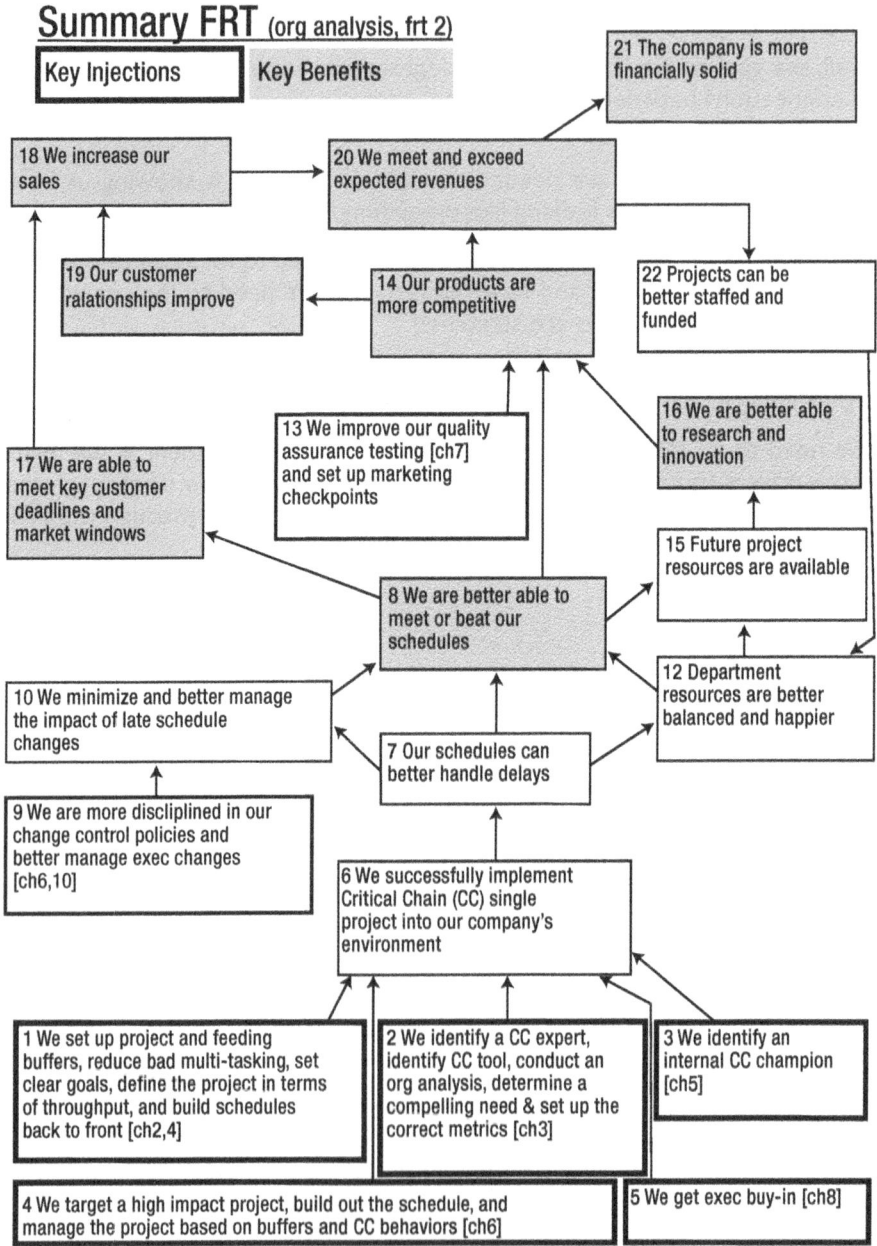

"So a few quick additions: 13) we add marketing checkpoints per my discussion with Ashley and with 14) better products, which helps 19) our customer relationships improve. With 20) better revenues we can also make sure 22) projects are better staffed. Then we can add 5) we need to get Exec buy-in as well."

"Whoa Tim, slow down. How about a short summary?"

"Sure. We put boxes 1-5 in place to help us successfully implement the Critical Chain. With the 6) Critical Chain in place, we can 7) better handle delays. If we can 9) put better change control in, we won't flood the system with work. With 6) better schedules, 13) better QA, our products will be better 14). In addition, with 6) better schedules, 16) we will have more time to innovate and that will get us 14) better products as well. With 14) better products and 8) better schedules customers will be happier, we will hit deadlines, and revenues will increase."

"Well, it sounds much better. We have worked on boxes 1-5 to put Critical Chain into place. With Phoenix and talking to Gary, I can see the schedules getting better. We just need time to see those results carry over to meeting the deadlines and happy customers. So yes, I can see we are getting there Tim. Interesting to see how it is all laid out here in your happy tree diagram. It will be interesting to see how well Micky will buy in to your plan, but real results on Phoenix will certainly get his attention."

"We'll my meeting is coming up with Micky shortly. Let's grab some coffee and then we can strategize from there." Tim suggests.

CHAPTER 9

Almost

Randal finds Tim in his new cube just before his meeting with Micky. "So Tim, what is the plan?"

"Same as with Grant."

"Seems a bit simple, Tim."

"True. With Grant, I highlighted the meet original commitments issues and the engineering concerns since that is his area of expertise. With Micky, it will be better to highlight the 'grow the business' aspects such as customer relationships and meeting revenues issues."

"That part makes sense. Be sure to highlight their areas of ownership and interest."

"Possibly this time I'll start with the cloud versus the issues as well."

"Eh? You are being TOC cryptic again, Tim."

"Cater to the audience. With Grant he lives a lot of the engineering issues, so it made sense to start the discussion there. Micky is the CEO and sees and lives the company's struggles, so starting with the cloud of the company's conflict should work well for him."

"Fair enough. Any other prep; we went through a lot of details for Grant?"

"Nope, we did all of the ground work and analysis already. I think we're good to go."

"Do you need me to be your wingman on this one?"

© Eric Bergland 2016
E. Bergland, *Get it Done On Time!*, DOI 10.1007/978-1-4842-1860-0_9

"I have been going a bit back and forth on that one, Randal. You certainly know the organization more so that would help. At the same time you also noted that Micky will be more open one on one. I need him to feel comfortable and I need to know where he stands. So probably best for me to go solo this time around."

"Okay, I have a few meetings this afternoon. Why don't we catch up tomorrow morning and we can review how things went and continue preparations for the Exec meeting."

"Sure."

Tim Meets with Micky

The next day, Tim walks up to Micky's office. As he enters he sees Micky finishing up a call just before he waves Tim to come in. Micky is over 6 foot, well built, and dressed impeccably.

"Hi Tim, it is nice to meet with you," Micky states, sizing Tim up.

"Hi Micky, it is good to meet with you as well."

"So I have been having regular meetings with Randal and he has indicated that you have been working with engineering to try and improve our process."

"That is correct; I have been looking through the different issues and see what we can do."

"And what have you seen?" Micky pausing to see what Tim comes up with.

Step 1: Show the Cloud

"I see that everyone wants the company to be successful. On one side we are obligated to meet existing contract commitments [crt 5]."

"True," agrees Micky.

"On the other side the competition is catching up and we need to grow revenues. This causes us to feel the need and pressure to focus on new requests and grow the business [crt 8]."

"Also very true."

"We have enough resources to meet existing commitments [crt 4], but not enough to meet existing commitments and grow the company at the same time. So we oscillate back and forth trying to meet these two needs."

Micky takes a short breath and, giving Tim some more time to see where he is going with this, he responds, "That certainly sums up a few of our challenges, Tim. So what do you suggest we do?"

Step 2: Blame the System and Highlight Key Issues from CRT

"The current product development system is not working for us. We run into schedule delays, cut quality to meet deadlines, and miss customer deadlines. This is all impacting the company's revenues and our ability to move forward to the extent that contract revenues are down 30%."

"Yes, revenues are down," Micky states, a little frustrated and waiting for Tim to finish his pitch.

Step 3: Introduce the Key Injection and Vision

Tim continues, "We need a new system. A system that can better accommodate our needs, support the original commitments, allow growth, has better change control, and allow us to deliver on-time. The Critical Chain project management system can get us there."

"This is the project management system that Grant and Gary have been working on for Phoenix?"

"Yes. We developed a stronger schedule, designed it to get revenues faster, and built it to better absorb reasonable delays and changes."

"And what about the other projects we have going on?" asks Micky.

"We can take the process and lessons from Phoenix and carry them over to the other projects."

"How long until we get results? What types of results can I expect, Tim?"

"As the projects execute, we can see that they are holding to their overall deadlines. We can also see them accommodate some of the customer and Exec changes better, but we have to use good change control to be very selective of the changes we choose. As the project's finish up, we should see them reaching their revenues sooner and the customers more engaged and happier."

"Tim, Phoenix is months out. The other projects are even farther out." Micky's patience is running out and his voice raising slightly. "We need *something* to go to the customers *now*. I can't go back to them with engineering promises of things getting better in half a year. We have done that already and our deliveries and quality got worse not better. We've lost a few key accounts and the others are not doing much better. I need something better to turn things around."

Tim stirs uncomfortably. "We have made the schedules much better and we have made the process significantly better for Phoenix. It *is* running better. It *will* help out the company. But it will take time for products to get developed. That part I can't control."

Micky sighs and sits back in his chair putting his hands down on his desk. "I can't just tell our customers to buy more from us based on the fact that we have just tweaked our process and we expect everything will be better in a few months. We have already been down that road. I am also concerned about getting everyone's hopes falsely stirred up if your new process can't fix our immediate problems."

Tim is a bit shocked, but he tries to recover. "Critical Chain can get us there, but we need to give it time. I can share results other organizations have gotten, but it takes time."

"That is the concern, Tim. We have run out of time. Maybe Critical Chain could get us there. Gary and Grant seem to think it shows promise. But engineering has promised changes time and time again. They make incremental improvements, yet we keep falling behind our deliveries and our competition is catching up. We need a game-changer Tim and I need it today. If engineering can't provide it then I will," Micky states a bit more defiant and resolved.

Tim and Micky sit there quietly for a moment. Micky is comfortable and defiantly holding the silence. Then Tim wants to end on some positive action going forward, "I'll keep working with Gary on the schedule and we can bring the results to the Exec meeting. We can highlight how we have improved and how we are staying on track."

Micky pauses, "Sure Tim. That sounds reasonable." Looking at his watch, he says, "Tim, I have a call coming up."

"Sure. Thank you for your time," and with that, Tim left Micky's office starting to think about how things went and what next steps would make sense."

Next Steps

The next morning things seem a bit somber. Randal had called and wanted to meet over at the company coffee shop right away. Tim was still thinking about how things had gone during his talk with Micky.

As Tim walks over to the coffee shop, surprisingly, Randal is already there at a table.

"Let's go for a walk, Tim."

"Sure." They quietly walk down the hall and out the building. Randal is looking very somber and turns to Tim.

"I found out Micky's next step this morning."

"Oh?" replies Tim.

"Micky cut your consulting contract effective immediately. He wants you to clean out your desk and be gone. Something about us being tight on money and budget cutting, but all of us know it is just a ruse. You must of really pushed his buttons somehow."

Tim stops walking for a second and takes everything in. "Actually, it didn't feel that way. As soon as I said we needed to improve the product development process and it would take time, he was done."

"Hmm, before you started consulting, engineering has been in the hot seat for months and has made a lot of promises. Micky took those promises to the customers. But then the promises didn't work out and Micky had to back pedal. Possibly this was the last straw."

"Possibly. I guess. Either way he was not open to the direction I was going unless I could guarantee results instantly. He seemed to have already made up his mind before we even started talking. At this point in time, I think I could have said anything and it would not have mattered."

"We can figure something out, Tim. Maybe you just caught Micky on an off day. Both Gary and I want to appeal his decision to end your contract. Grant was a bit surprised by Micky's actions as well. He said he would look into it, but that no matter what we did, it was not going to get resolved before the Exec meeting."

Tim changing the subject, "So what are you and Gary going to do about the Exec meeting?"

"We will continue to gather the results. So far they are looking promising. As expected, we've hit a number of issues, consumed some of the project buffer, and we're still on track to hit our deliverables. The team feels more confident that the schedule is realistic and they actually have a chance to succeed. I have been working with Gary to talk with the customers to better enable a clean feature check-out. The customers appreciate the attention and Gary feels it will help us get payments a month early if the schedules continue to hold up."

"That sounds very good, Randal."

"It was all from your help and support, Tim. I have also taken items from our discussion with Grant and I'll see if I can work them into the presentation as well. Although with the Exec review it is more of a status update then a buy-in discussion. If I need help, is it okay to call you Tim?"

"Sure, of course."

"Seems like you have a little bit of a break until we can get something sorted out," Randal notes.

"I guess I need to get back to updating and sending out my resume again," Tim says, trailing off.

"Gary and I will work with Grant. We will see if we can figure something out. You have put a lot of time and heart to help out our company. It really has made a difference."

CHAPTER 10

Board Room Meeting

Gary and Randal enter the board room. It has a large oak oval table surrounded by over 20 overstuffed chairs. Actual paintings, not prints, adorn the walls. A side bar of ice water with lemons, three types of coffee, and pastries sits off to the side. Gary looks nervously at Randal, "It has been a while since I last visited this room."

Randal looks back, "It is the first time I've been here." They go off to the side and pick two chairs next to each other. Shortly thereafter Ashley (the marketing and sales director), Herb (HR), and Grant (COO) walk in and take their places. Micky enters the room, pauses to look around, and enters as if it is friendly surroundings and sits next to Ashley. Then Clint, Neal, and Bryn enter. They are the company's three external board members. Clint was the CEO and Neal was the president of their respective software companies. Bryn was a founder of a software start-up that went from five employees to 150 before she solid it off for a small fortune.

Randal watches as Bryn approaches the podium. "So for this quarter's board meeting, we have three agenda items. Grant will go over the current financials, Gary and Randal will discuss the engineering status, and Micky will review strategy and direction. At the end, we can cover any additional opens people have." She looks around the room, and seeing no concerns about the agenda, she says, "Okay, then, Grant please provide your financial overview."

Chapter 10 | Board Room Meeting

Grant approaches the podium and starts walking through various numbers, charts, and diagrams covering ROI, burn rates, revenues, and company reserves. Randal's eyes go blurry, but he tunes back in when Grant goes on to say, "We are in a tight spot. We cannot sustain the company based on our current revenues. Bottom line, we must change and quickly." The board members ask a few clarifying questions with seriousness in their tone, but at the same time, it does not seem to be news to them. This had been going on for a while.

Randal leans over to Gary and whispers, "This is serious."

Gary replies, "Yes, we have tried several things in the past, but the results have not been compelling enough. That is why Tim's Critical Chain caught my and Grant's attention. It was something new, with a track record, and the more we worked with it, the more it made sense. It wasn't easy, but it made a difference to both engineering and the company as a whole."

"So if the issues are serious and have been going on for a while, I can see why Micky has been freaking out. This is his first time as acting CEO and I'm sure he does not want the company to fail in his first year. It would look terrible. And considering he killed Tim's contract I can see that he is not bought into Critical Chain. So he has to be stressed."

"Then why does he look so confident?" inquires Gary.

"I have no idea, Gary, but it makes me nervous."

Grant finishes his presentation and steps down from the podium. Bryn speaks up, "Gary and Randal, the engineering update please." Randal and Gary then walk over to the podium.

Gary and Randal Present

Gary carefully approaches the microphone. "We have made great progress with engineering. The Phoenix project has made significant improvements. The teams are more focused. The schedules we have created are more complete, solid, and reliable than before. The QA plans are more complete and flexible as well. We are 30% ahead and on track to finish our first customer milestone early."

Micky looks over to Ashley. "Gary," Ashley speaking up, "We have heard engineering promises before. How do we know this is sustainable and not just going to fall apart like some of the past attempts?"

Randal steps in, "That is a good question, Ashley. We have implemented a new project management process with the help of a consultant. With his help, we put new systems into place. Captured the process and learnings so we can share it with other development teams. The system allows us to manage our schedules and protect our deadlines as long as we stay disciplined. The process itself has a good track record with helping other organizations as well."

"What about the recent Phoenix feature requests you tried to rejected from marketing? From our customers?" she continued.

Gary looked over to Ashley, "We built out our schedules to hit the timelines marketing provided. We absorbed some of the requests, but other requests would require us to push out the schedule and marketing did not want us to do that."

Micky stepped in from there, "If we cannot respond to urgent customer requests then we lose their favor and future contracts."

"I think we all agree," said Randal trying to channel Tim, "We all want the company to be successful. We need to both support our current requests as well as be willing to take additional requests. But if we take on more requests than we can realistically support, we will miss the schedules and that will not help anyone."

Micky stares coldly at Randal for a few moments. The room sits quiet. "You still have not answered the sustainability question. You say things are on track now. How do we know if things will remain on track?" Micky asks, poking the engineering results a bit more.

Randal looks at Gary. "We have a new process in place. A sustainable process," Gary replies.

"How long until we know for sure?" inquires Micky a bit coldly.

"We are making progress with Phoenix. We're ahead of the next milestone. The final delivery is in a few months. So it will be very clear then. From there we can continue the process and any knowledge we have from it to the next project."

"So it will be months to know for sure for Phoenix and even longer for the other projects. We're tight on funds. We have had engineering problems before. But you think it will be *okay*." Micky emphasizing the word okay and looks around the board room.

After a long moment of silence Grant steps in, "Gary and Randal I do not believe some of the board members are familiar with this new process. Can you summarize it for them?"

"Sure Grant," states Randal. "The new process is focused on creating banks of time to manage and protect our project deadlines, reducing inefficient multi-tasking, and building more robust schedules that will help us reach our revenues sooner. The better managed schedules will benefit us by helping to reduce employee burnout, address more customer requests, and help with maintaining and gaining new contracts."

Chapter 10 | Board Room Meeting

The board members nod and ask several clarifying questions that both Gary and Randal cover. Grant then asks, "So Gary and Randal, do you have confidence in this process?"

"Yes," They both agree.

Grant also steps in, "Tim, the consultant Gary and Randal hired, walked me through this new product development process. I was pretty impressed with it. As Randal said, it will help us manage our schedules better and more reliably. At the same time, Tim showed me how it can help us grow the company. With some key items the new process and stronger schedules will enable us to meet our existing commitments as well as *some* of the urgent customer requests and late changes marketing needs to improve our relationships with customers. As Gary noted, the results on Phoenix are solid and we can transfer this process to other projects. So I believe we can turn the company around using this methodology, but as Micky noted, it will take time. We have some benefits to Phoenix. It will not take a lot, but it will take some time to start rolling it onto other projects and in turn start seeing benefits there as well."

Bryn looks around. "Thank you Gary, for the update. Any other questions at this time?" Ashley looks over at Micky and he gives a dismissive sideways head nod no. Seeing no additional questions, Bryn states, "Micky your update on strategy and direction."

Micky Presents

Micky confidently walks up to the podium, "We're on the Titanic and heading for an iceberg. We either change course and do something different or the whole ship goes down. We're not delivering the products our customers need when they need it. We're losing contracts and barely making money on the contracts we have. We keep hearing the same story over and over—engineering needs more resources, more time—yet it keeps missing its deadlines. We do not have the time or funds to keep waiting. We simply cannot survive this way." Micky lets the statement stand... "I want to increase the marketing budget by 20% and aggressively push into the market and make our products stand out and distinguish ourselves from our competitors."

Everyone pauses. Grant is the first to speak, "Micky, where do we get the funds? We are already maxed out."

"We outsource engineering. I have already talked to several software organizations in China. We can get same development work done at a fraction of the cost. They are familiar with our markets and they have an *actual* record of delivering on time," Micky says, emphasizing the word actual.

The execs and board look shocked. Micky stands there gleaming. "I have already started the preliminary contracts; we could turn this over to them in a matter of weeks. Free ourselves from the engineering deadweight that is pulling us down and come out stronger and faster than before."

Gary is the first to speak, "Micky, they don't know our technology."

"I have already talked to them. They have already worked in similar areas. We would need to retain some local technical experts and they can help ramp them up and get familiar with our existing code base."

"What about our intellectual property? You outsource our development then you are outsourcing our intellectual property. We would be completely dependent on the other company. I've heard of less scrupulous organizations taking funds and developing products for one company and then turning around and selling the same products to their competitors. Something like that would cripple us," states Neal.

"We would have to put safeguards in place. I've talked with peers at other organizations and know which companies to steer clear of," Micky states confidently.

"What about the local engineers? We have already invested heavily in training them and getting them to use to our code base," Gary asks, concerned.

"We would lay off the majority of them and keep a core team of architects to help guide and manage the work in China. We have to change course. This will get us there. It will be at a fraction of the current development cost and they have a successful track record of delivering products. We can get our pipeline of products quickly and reliably on track, expand it, and aggressively market it. We will be significantly better off than we have ever been," Micky states soundly and confidently.

The board and execs look around. Bryn speaks up, "Clint, you have some outsourcing experience. What is your take on it?"

Clint thinks for a moment. "We certainly did some outsourcing in my organization, but we phased it in. As Micky noted, the cost savings can be significant; that is why so many organizations look into it. The coordination has to be really well done. There is also ramp-up time. And as Micky noted, you need to find a really good company to work with. And as Neal noted, you have to watch your intellectual property with any place you outsource. You don't want to give them too much. Overall it's an interesting proposition Micky brings up. It has some real strengths to it and some really big concerns as well."

Then Bryn steps in to lead the meeting, "As Micky pointed out and the updates Grant presented we can't just stick with what we have been doing. We have to change something. We have two very different directions to consider. We can try and trust that engineering will continue to make great progress soon enough or, as Micky said, we can try and change the game all together and outsource. To make this decision, we need to review each option more deeply and then as a group decide."

Board Review

The board dismisses Gary, Randal, and Ashley and convenes to review the decision. As the three of them wait, they see a man in his late 50s approach the board room and enter. Gary does a double take and then turns to Randal, "Randal, that was Roger. He is our CEO who had temporarily stepped down and let Micky step up as interim CEO."

"Really? Interesting. I wonder what they asked him here for."

"I'm not sure…" Looking over to Ashley, she seemed puzzled as well.

After a long hour and half everyone was invited back in. Bryn stands at the podium. "Gary, you have made great progress. If you had just brought promises again, the board wouldn't believe you. You brought data, results, and a solid plan to move ahead. Grant spoke very highly of your consultant Tim and how he thought your plan had been worked out not just to help engineering, but to grow the company." Gary nodded.

She continued, "Micky, true to your reputation you have brought a great and bold plan to radically change things and get us to a much better position quickly. But it also comes with great risks both in how fast and successfully it would work and it potentially puts our intellectual property at risk." Micky holds himself confidently.

"This is not a winner-takes-all decision. We need what is best for the company and its future," Bryn emphatically states. "The board has decided to very carefully monitor Phoenix and we want a monthly report and review of its status and progress. We also want to see this new Critical Chain methodology and learnings rolled out to additional projects as quickly as possible. In the past, we have had cost over runs, excessive overtime, customer delay penalties, and customer penalties for incomplete features. These have combined to drag our overall company financials down. Per Grant's estimates, Phoenix will beat its original revenue estimates, deliver on time, and meet the required customer requirements. If we can carry this success forward and to the other projects, this will enable us to increase our overall revenues, improve and grow our customer relations, and turn around and grow the company. Gary, your team has done very well, but we definitely need and expect this progress to continue."

"Understood."

Bryn continues, "Micky. Under a very challenging situation you have done well and continued to innovate. Roger has indicated that he intends to formally step down due his medical concerns and we thank him for all of his accomplishments and sharing his insights about our current situation. Micky, you will need to continue to work with Grant to leverage and successfully sell and market Phoenix's success. You *and* Grant will work as co-CEO's to move us forward. Grant will continue to focus on operations and engineering. Micky, you will be promoted to co-CEO immediately and will continue to drive the company's overall marketing strategy and customer relationships. Once the company stabilizes, we can possibly revisit outsourcing as a way to expand and extend our existing development efforts. But we need to get the 'here and now' stable before we can look too far forward. You will need to work with and leverage Grant and Gary's technical expertise if we are to be successful."

Micky looks over warily to Gary, "Understood."

"Any remaining questions or open topics for this forum?" inquires Bryn. Looking around the room and seeing everyone quiet, she continues. "Good. Then that concludes this quarter's meeting."

Epilog

A few days, Gary, Randal, and Tim reconnect at the coffee shop where Tim first saw Randal. They filled Tim in on what came out of the board meeting.

Tim looks over to Randal, somewhat baiting him, "So who won?"

Randal looks a bit puzzled, "In some ways I want to say engineering. But honesty I'm not sure; it seems like everyone got something."

Tim smiles, "I would go along with what Bryn said as far as the company winning. It is less of one department out-doing the other. It's more about the company as a whole doing better." Tim looks at Gary, "Looks like you saved the engineering team from outsourcing."

"True, Tim. I realize now that I needed your and Randal's help to do it. We had done some improvements here and there but the processes we have now work much better. "

"Tim helped us look past the symptoms of our issues and figure out where the root of our problems are and where we needed to focus our efforts," Randal states.

Gary looks a bit oddly at Randal, "You are starting to sound like Tim."

"Umm, possibly he rubbed off on me. But I definitely dress better," Randal says with a smile.

Chapter 10 | Board Room Meeting

Gary continues, "With Critical Chain, Phoenix is launching on time, with the required features, and we should achieve the customer sign-off significantly faster than our past projects. With Grant's help and new position we have balanced out marketing's sudden feature requests and been able to put in a stronger change control process [frt 9]. We are also in the process of rolling it out to other projects."

"That sounds great, Gary."

"And Randal, your take on Micky's promotion?"

"Umm, I think it is more politics. Sure it's called a promotion, but Micky is not *the* CEO or at least the only CEO. They moved engineering away from him and Grant kept operations. It was clear that Micky had grown to resent the engineering team. He is exceptionally good at what he is good at and not so good at what he isn't. They want to keep him focused on marketing and customer relations. He knows our market and has long-standing relations with customers. It's something that the board and to my understanding Roger underscored. The company could not risk or survive losing Micky and the customer relationships he has built up and cultivated over the years."

"And the outsourcing, Gary?"

"It was Micky's idea. He talked to a few people and really latched onto the idea, but he had oversimplified the technical challenges involved. As the board said definitely something we can't do now, but Grant mentioned in a year or two that we might consider outsourcing some of the non-proprietary development to help extend our existing development [frt 11]. We really need to get our current projects under control before we can even consider it."

"And Tim," Randal interjects, "Now that Grant has reopened your consulting contract as well as an opportunity to join full time, what do you win?"

"I get to keep working with you guys," Tim says with a big smile.

"True true," say Randal and Gary, both laughing.

"But Tim, with Critical Chain implemented in Phoenix and the process documented so we can carry it over to other projects, what will you focus on?" inquires Randal.

"Ahh Randal, we have implemented a single project Critical Chain to help each project do well. Once we have got it down and things are running well, we can next look at Critical Chain multi-project to help the organization manage multiple parallel projects effectively [frt 21]."

"I see," says Randal jokingly, "More theories, concepts, and terminology for Gary and me to learn."

"It isn't that bad, is it?"

Randal turns to look at Tim, "Well one last thing Tim, in regards to your office cube. I seem to have run into a bit of a delay...."

Final Future Reality Tree (FRT)

Tim, ever reviewing and tuning his plan, adds two last items to his FRT.

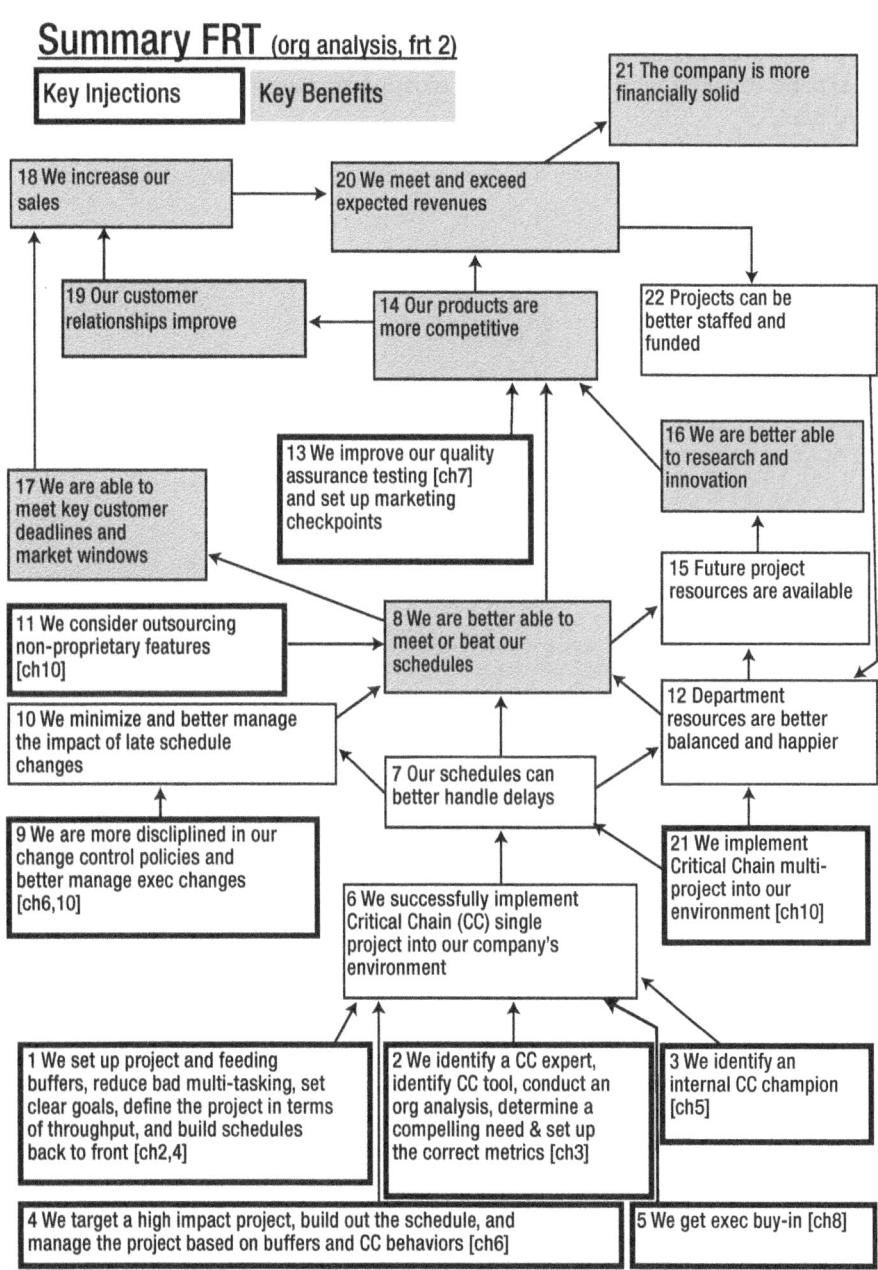

Chapter 10 | Board Room Meeting

The future needs to 21) look at Critical Chain multi-project and the possible consideration of 11) outsourcing non-proprietary features. Then he stands back and says to himself, "Now that looks a bit more complete. We have 6) Critical Chain in place as our foundation, 9) change control to pace new requests, 13) a better QA process, and 21) Critical Chain multi-project as we move forward. We also have a future possibility to 11) outsource some work to expand capacity without impacting existing resources. Now that is a more solid plan."

APPENDIX A

Key Concepts

Chapter 1: Introductions

- Critical Chain can be used to help deliver projects faster and more reliably.

- Theory of Constraints (TOC) is a set of general problem-solving tools that can be used to look at an organization as a whole, identify areas to focus on, and drive overall improvements. It can be used help focus teams on any improvement effort from Critical Chain, Scrum, Agile, new technology deployments, and so on.

Chapter 2: High-Level Critical Chain Overview

Critical Chain is a Theory of Constraints solution that addresses the common problems found in project management so you can better plan, manage, and be more successful with projects.

Theory of Constraints (TOC) is a general problem-solving model that can be applied to a variety of environments, but it has one fundamental concept. In looking at any kind of system such as project management, manufacturing, or distribution, you can find one constraint that is limiting the overall system. If you focus improvement efforts on this constraint, the whole system will benefit and the bottom line of the organization will improve.

Common project-management *issues* Critical Chain can help address:

- Projects miss critical deadlines and market opportunities [crt 25]

- You cut too many key features to make deadlines [crt 19]

- Your products are not competitive enough (due to slow project turnaround, missing deadlines, and cutting key features) [crt 23]
- There is too much resource burn-out and turnover [crt 14]
- You go over budget due to project overruns and do not make expected revenues our product lines [crt 26]
- There are internal projects fights over shared resources [crt 18]

Possible Critical Chain *benefits*:

- On-time delivery of products significantly improves [frt 8]
- You are able to complete projects much faster [frt 8]
- Hidden or misused resource capacity is surfaced [frt 12]
- The company and its products are more competitive [frt 14]
- The company is more profitable [frt 20]

For sample results, see these web sites for the latest results:

- Avraham Goldratt Institute (AGI): www.goldratt.com
- Goldratt's Marketing Group: www.toc-goldratt.com
- Realization case studies: www.realization.com
- ProChain success stories: www.prochain.com
- Theory of Constraints International Certification Organization: www.tocico.org

Key Critical Chain components that help you get results are:

- Project buffers to better manage task variability [frt 1]
- Reducing bad multi-tasking to find hidden and misused resource capacity [frt 1]
- Building schedules (back-to-front) and challenging assumptions [frt 1]
- Organizational analysis (TOC TP) to better understand our overall project environment (creating the CRT and FRT)

You can mix project-management methodologies (Critical Chain, Scrum, Agile, etc.), but you really need to have a solid grounding in each of the methodologies you are trying to mix. If you want to learn more about combining Lean, Six Sigma, and TOC, you can look at the TOC book *Velocity*.

Chapter 3: Factors for Success

Successful implementations ideally have:

- A certified Critical Chain implementation expert who really understands the mechanics of the Critical Chain solution, including how to use it to improve the organization's throughput and how to successfully implement it in an organization.
- Someone who has Critical Chain software tool experience.
- For complicated and political environments, someone who is certified Theory of Constraints Thinking Process background who can complete an organizational analysis.
- An organization with a compelling need and desire to change.
- Metrics that encourage desired behaviors.

Some of the environmental issues to consider can include the following:

- Does the organization's project team take ownership of the Critical Chain solution?
- Is senior management on board with the solution? The other way of looking at it is your organization independent and isolated enough that you can set up and manage schedules how you want, without senior management involvement as long as you deliver products successfully?
- How complex is your project environment? Single project? Matrixed multi-project?
- Does the organization have good or poor project-management practices?

The better the organization understands Critical Chain and the characteristics and factors mentioned, the better you can help move the implementation along as well as make sure the person you have helping implement it in your organization is covering everything needed.

Chapter 4: Concepts

Key CCPM benefits that help you get results are:

- Project and feeding buffers to better manage variability
- Reducing bad multi-tasking to find hidden or misused resource capacity
- Building schedules back-to-front challenging assumptions
- Organizational Analysis (TOC TP) to better understand your environment

The Organizational Analysis (TOC TP) can help you:

- Understand the organizational environment and constraints that limit your success
- Understand the issues, how they interconnect, and what the core drivers are
- Understand how Critical Chain can help you address these issues
- Understand what outside of Critical Chain is needed to ensure your success

Chapter 5: Championing Ideas

- Just having a good idea by itself does not make things happen; you often need someone who can help champion the idea through the organization. This person needs to meet with key stakeholders to identify the benefits for their area, identify the concerns they have for their area, and work to minimize these concerns. The champion also needs to understand the organization's approval process and drive the idea through this process in the most efficient way possible.
- In addition to having external Critical Chain expertise to help you implement the Critical Chain solution, it is advisable to have an internal Critical Chain champion to help drive the implementation, work on key stakeholder concerns and issues, and navigate the organization's adoption process.

- The TOC Cloud tool can be helpful in looking at conflicts to find unique ways to resolve them.
  - For day-to-day conflicts, the clouds from the Management Skills Workshop (MSW) can be helpful.
  - For organizational conflicts in complex environments, it is important to look at the TOC Thinking Process in addition to the cloud to fully develop solutions and implementation plans.
- The TOC cloud is composed of the following pieces:
  - The *common goal* both sides share (A)
  - The *needs* each side has (B, C)
  - The *wants* each side is verbalizing that are being driven by the wants (D, D')
- The assumptions you should commonly challenge on the cloud are:
  - The true conflict between both sides' wants (DD')
  - Each side's connection between the need and want (BD, CD')

Chapter 6: Implementation Steps

Phoenix Setup:

- When looking at moving an organization onto Critical Chain ideally, you should try to move the whole organization. If time is an issue then you can look at staggering the implementation and pick one or two high-impact projects to focus on. They need to have a bottom-line impact as well and cannot be side projects since the effort needed and results created would not be taken seriously.
- If necessary, it is possible to intercept a project already in process and simply build the new Critical Chain schedule from where the project is currently at to the end.

- To really make a culture change in an organization, you need three things:
  - Top management buy-in and agreement to lead the charge
  - Determine key measurement changes that will incentivize the desired behaviors of the new culture
  - Education for all involved, including the new measurements.

Phoenix Network Build:

- As part of the network build, it is important that the managers and the team learn the key Critical Chain concepts [Chapters 2 and 4 items].
- You want to be sure to build the project to throughput (where you generate income or further the goals of the organization).
- When you build the schedule, you look at the project's goal and build backward using the phrasing *in order to.. we must..* and add in any dependencies.
- When you need to compress and tighten a schedule up, look at BORA: Break a link, Overlap tasks, Reduce scope or duration, or Add a resource.

Phoenix Execution:

- As you execute the schedule, the team should have regular, typically weekly, schedule updates. As part of these updates, the project manager and the team should review the fever chart for the different project and endpoint/milestone buffers. The fever chart measures how much buffer you have consumed compared to how much of the project you have completed. Green means you are on track, yellow means you are falling behind and need to look at ways to recover, and red means that you are putting the project deadline at risk and need to act to add time back into the buffer.
- To add time back into the buffer, review BORA: Break a link, Overlap tasks, Reduce scope or duration, or Add a resource.
- As you execute the project, there are several behaviors you'll want to be sure to maintain. These were covered in Chapters 2 and 4. Some of these behaviors include:

- Roadrunner: You encourage people to work as quickly as they can.
- Relay race: You encourage people to cleanly hand off work to the next resource (dependency) as quickly as possible.
- Reduce bad multi-tasking: You want to avoid any multi-tasking that stretches out work and delays hand-offs.
- Management does not beat up resources for missing focused times, the focus times are aggressive by design so you should expect that several will be missed. You'll want to manage the overall project buffer and overall deadline, not micro-manage resources.

Phoenix Post-Mortem Plan:

1. POOGI stands for the Process Of OnGoing Improvement. Once you have set up a new process, you need to maintain and continue to improve upon it.

Micky's Urgent Requests:

1. Even when you set up Critical Chain, it is not foolproof. If you let too much work into the system, you will flood it. So you must have good discipline and manage a good change control process.
2. If you know you will always have changes at key points in the schedule, you should try to minimize these changes (i.e., change control) as well as proactively reserve capacity for these changes.

Chapter 7: Ambitious Targets

- When people put together a plan for a project, they often focus on the tasks involved. For example, the QA tests that need to be identified and run. The ambitious target tool can help you look broader. You can clarify the goals of the overall project and identify issues and concerns that the team has in general based on past experience as well as in trying to meet the project's goal.

- The Ambitious target tool allows you to successfully use an individual's innate ability to complain in a constructive way to find ways to address concerns and make the project more successful.
- Key steps in creating an Ambitious target include:
  1. Define a goal that is clear, concise, and measurable.
  2. Have the team identify issues and concerns in trying to reach the specific goal, leveraging past experience when possible.
  3. Develop suggestions (sometimes called *intermediate objectives*) to address each issue. Make sure that the team feels confident that the suggestions can successfully help them reach the goal. If not, review the additional issues and develop additional suggestions.
  4. Sequence the suggestions into a tangible plan that is regularly tracked.
  5. When reading ambitious targets, use *in order to* (above item) *we must* (below item). For example, *in order to reach the goal of shipping a product that meets the QA customer release criteria, we must detail out the QA customer release criteria*.

Chapter 8: Individual Buy-In

- The six layers of resistance give you a systematic framework on how you can organize your analysis (CRT, FRT, etc.).
- The buy-in process is how you *conversationally* walk through someone through your analysis and the layers of resistance to get their understanding and potential acceptance.

The six layers of resistance:

- Layer 1: Lack of consensus on the problem.
- Layer 2: People do not agree on the direction of the solution.
- Layer 3: Arguing the proposed solution cannot yield the desired outcome.
- Layer 4: Yes, *but*. Concerns about potential negative side-effects from proposed solution.

- Layer 5: Obstacles that stand in the way of implementing solution into the environment.
- Layer 6: Raising doubts, wait and see, unverbalized fears.

How to approach each layer:

- Layer 1: Lack of consensus on the problem.
  - *Pre-work*: Build out the CRT for the organization to understand the issues, how they interconnect, and the core problem driving the issues.
  - *Buy-in*: Pick a few key issues that resonate with that person's area and the organization as a whole and work to quantify their impact. Then verbally walk through how they are interconnected.
    - Don't show the CRT or FRT to people (at least not the first meeting). It tends to overwhelm and frustrate people not familiar with TOC. It's just like showing a page of calculus formulas to someone who doesn't know calculus and saying, "isn't this great"!
- Layer 2: People do not agree on the direction of the solution.
  - *Pre-work*: Focus on the core conflict and the key injection(s) necessary to break it.
  - *Buy-in:* Review the cloud by showing or verbally walking through the conflict. Then work with the person to realize (better) or reveal to them the key injection. Then promptly move onto Layer 3 to justify why the injection addresses the issues of the organization.
- Layer 3: Arguing the proposed solution cannot yield the desired outcome.
  - *Pre-work*: Build out the organization's FRT.
  - *Buy-in*: Start with the key injection and verbally walk through and show how the key injection leads to and is connected to several of the key benefits of the FRT. Cover just the key benefits that the person you are talking will find of value; there is no need or value to cover them all.

- Layer 4: Yes, but. Concerns about potential side-effects from proposed solution.
  - *Pre-work*: If possible, try to anticipate negative effects from your suggested direction. Then try to come up with recommendations that negate these issues if they come up. The negative branch (NBR) TOC tool is typically used for these issues.
  - *Buy-in*: Be patient and be ready to address any concerns raised.
- Layer 5: Obstacles that stand in the way of implementing solution into the environment.
  - *Pre-work*: If possible, try to anticipate any potential obstacles and how they could be overcome.
  - *Buy-in*: Be patient and ready to address any concerns raised.
- Layer 6: Raising doubts, wait and see, unverbalized fears.
  - *Pre-work*: Be aware of this challenge and look for ways to address it.
  - *Buy-in*: As you get buy-in, work to get commitments and timelines for people to act.
    - If you find some people are holding back, try to see what their concerns are. Work to surface any "yes, but" concerns and obstacles then work to address them.
    - If people seem to be holding back and it seems more driven by fear and doubt, work with them to see the pain with the current process and the value in moving to the new process.
- Be sure to focus blame on the system. Avoid finger pointing and focus on the system and how the way it operates is holding the company back.
- Be sure to close the deal. For an initial or exec meeting, layers 1-3 are good. Always be sure to close the deal and get some commitment at the end of the meeting (otherwise, why did you hold the meeting in the first place?). Address the remaining layers (yes..but, obstacles, etc.) as they come up or in subsequent meetings.

Chapter 9: Almost

- Randal and Tim Prep:
    - Once you have created the CRT, FRT, and your plan to address the six layers of resistance, you are ready to start working with people to get their buy-in. You just have to tailor what you present based on your audience by highlighting and focusing on the issues that relate to that specific person's area of interest. You can start the conversation with issues or with the cloud. It depends on which one you think will better resonate with the person you are talking to.
- Next Steps:
    - Even when you have everything ready for the buy-in, some people may be more open to suggestions (like Grant) and others will be less open or will have their own and potentially competing suggestions (like Micky). There are no guarantees.

Chapter 10: Exec Review

- It is important to have executive buy-in, otherwise your implementation of Critical Chain could be blocked or hampered.
- Once you have single project Critical Chain implemented, the next step to consider is to look at Critical Chain multi-project to help manage multiple parallel projects effectively.

Chapter Questions
Chapter 1: Introductions
LivingTV:
    1. What happened to LivingTV?

Tim and Randal Reconnect:
    1. What is Critical Chain useful for?
    2. What is TOC useful for?

Chapter 2: High-Level Critical Chain Overview

What Is TOC and Critical Chain:

1. What is Critical Chain?
2. What is TOC?

Critical Chain Issues, Benefits, and Sample Results:

1. What are some of the common project-management issues Critical Chain can help address?
2. What are some of the Critical Chain benefits?

Key Parts of Critical Chain:

1. What are some of the key Critical Chain components that help us get results?

Project Buffers:

1. What do project buffers do?
2. What are some of the issues that can cause project variability?

Multi-Tasking:

1. What does reducing bad multi-tasking give you?
2. Is all multi-tasking bad?

Building Schedules:

1. What does building schedules back-to-front give you?

Organizational Analysis:

1. What is the benefit of an organizational analysis?

Multiple Methodologies:

1. What can influence the success of implementing a new project-management process even if it is a proven process?
2. Can you mix other project-management methodologies with Critical Chain?

CRT and FRT:

1. What does Tim's CRT/FRT flowcharts help with?
2. Is this something that should be shared with everyone?

Chapter 3: Factors for Success

Introductions:
> 1. What was Gary's feeling on how good the Critical Chain methodology was?
> 2. What was Tim's thinking on why Gary did not get very good results?

Key Characteristics of Successful Implementations:
> 1. Which areas are important for successful implementations? What is the benefit of each area?
> 2. If your company is already using Critical Chain, how well do you address the above areas for successful implementations?

Environmental Factors:
> 1. What four organizational issues can be important for successful implementations? For extra credit, explain why.
> 2. What other areas beyond this list do you see as critical for a successful implementation or a potential major issue that could de-rail an implementation?
> 3. If your company is already using Critical Chain, how well do you address the above organizational issues? Are there other issues that are a concern?

Chapter 4: How Does the Critical Chain Solution Work

Key Critical Chain Benefits:
> 1. What are the key Critical Chain benefits?

Project and Feeding Buffers, Padding Dates:
> 1. What does it mean to pad dates? Why can it be problematic?
> 2. What is the management and engineering poker game over?

Project and Feeding Buffers, Project Buffers:
1. What is the value of a project buffer? How is it different than management adding padding (additional time) to the team's deadline?
2. What are some of the behaviors that Critical Chain tries to implement to improve project performance? Briefly describe them.

Project and Feeding Buffers, Feeding Buffers:
1. What is the value of feeding buffers?

Project and Feeding Buffers, Safety Time:
1. What is safety time?

Project and Feeding Buffers, Managing Project Variability:
1. What does Critical Chain try to do in regard to variability? How?

Reducing Bad Multi-Tasking:
1. What does bad multi-tasking do to your deadlines, resource capacity, and responsiveness?

Defining the Project Goal and Building Schedules Back-to-Front:
1. What is the first step in building a schedule back-to-front?
2. What does the phrase *in order to (previous task) we must (successive task)* first help you with?
3. What does *in order to (goal) we must (and list out the key tasks in the schedule)* allow you to do?
4. Overall, how does building the schedule back-to-front help you?

Organizational Analysis:
1. How does Critical Chain and the organizational analysis work together to provide a more complete solution?
2. How does the organizational analysis help?

Chapter 5: Championing Ideas

LivingTV Interactive's Dilemma:
1. What was LivingTV's dilemma? What choice was it struggling with?
2. Why was LivingTV stuck?

Get it Done On Time!

LivingTV Interactive's Conflict Cloud:
1. What is the common goal that both sides share?
2. What are the wants of each side?
3. What are the needs driving the wants of each side?

Looking for Possible Resolutions:
1. Of the AB, BD, AC, CD', DD' connections, which three connections in the cloud does Tim try to challenge? Why those three specifically?

Spark of an Idea:
1. What link (AB, AC, BD, CD', DD') did Tim challenge?
2. What assumption did he identify that he was able to challenge?
3. How did breaking this assumption create a win-win solution for the company?

Initial Manager Meeting:
1. What was Tim trying to prevent by meeting with each of the directors before the Exec review?

Lobbying in Preparation for the Exec Review:
1. What did John, Mike, Bill, and Jim like about the pre-show concept?
2. What were John, Mike, Bill, and Jim's reservations about the pre-show concept?
3. How did their responses relate to each of their respective departments?
4. When pitching an idea, how would your approach change based on your audience?

The Exec Review:
1. How did Tim and Lori's work help in the Exec review?

Appendix

Chapter 6: Single Project Implementation Steps

Phoenix Setup:

1. What are two ways to implement Critical Chain into an organization? Which one is more ideal than the other?
2. Is it possible to intercept a project that is already in flight with Critical Chain?
3. To really make a culture change in an organization, what three things do you need?

Phoenix Network Build:

1. As part of the network build, does all of the team need to know the Critical Chain concepts?
2. What defines the end of the project?
3. What phrasing can you use when building out the schedule and checking dependencies?
4. What is BORA and what is it used for?
5. What are some of the issues that Tim, Gary, and Jeremy ran into when building out the Phoenix schedule?

Phoenix Execution:

1. How often should the team update the schedule?
2. What does the fever chart measure?
3. What do the different colors of the fever chart mean?
4. How can you recover time?
5. What are some of the key behaviors you want during project execution? See Chapters 2 and 4 for more details.

Phoenix Post-Mortem Plan:

1. What is POOGI and what is it for?

Micky's Urgent Requests:

1. What is the value of a change control process?
2. If you know you will always have changes at key points in the schedule, what are some of the possible options?

Chapter 7: Ambitious Targets

Background and QA Issues:
    1. What is the challenge faced by the QA team?

Define Your Goal:
    1. What criteria makes up a clear goal?

List Out Clear Issues and Their Impact:
    1. What issues are impacting QA?

Define Intermediate Objects (IOs):
    1. Who should be first to make suggestions to address an issue raised? Why?
    2. What are "flying pig" suggestions and why are they useful?
    3. At the end, Tim checks the suggestions that Nir and Anthony came up with against the goal. Why?

Sequence the Intermediate Objectives (IOs):
    1. What three things is Tim looking for from each suggestion?
    2. What does Ambitious Targets allow us to do over a task oriented schedule?
    3. What are the high-level steps in building an ambitious target?

Chapter 8: Individual Buy-In

Meeting with Sales and Marketing:
    1. What does Tim learn in talking with Ashley?

Meeting with Human Resources:
    1. What does Tim learn in talking with Herb?

Randal and Tim Prep for the Meeting with Grant:
    1. What are the six layers of resistance used for?
    2. What are the six layers of resistance?
    3. What TOC tools are used for the first four layers?
    4. Why is it bad to show the CRT/FRT and use TOC terminology when trying to get buy-in from someone not familiar with TOC?

5. Why is it important to blame the system?
6. Why bother with the organizational analysis, CRT, FRT, and getting all of the execs' to buy-in? Wouldn't it just be simpler to build the Critical Chain schedules, add the buffers, and implement it in engineering without the rest of the organization's involvement?
7. Why is it so important to close the deal?

Meeting with Grant:
1. What major stages does Tim go through in talking with Grant?
2. What areas does Tim go through when he walks through the vision (Layer 2) with Grant?
3. What does Tim learn in talking to Grant?

Chapter 9: Almost

Randal and Tim Prep:
1. What does Tim choose to focus on for his meeting with Micky compared to his meeting with Grant?

Tim Meets with Micky:
1. What three steps does Tim go through when presenting to Micky?
2. Would you have done anything different in meeting with Micky?

Next Steps:
1. What are some of the benefits Randal and Gary are seeing from implementing Critical Chain on the Phoenix project?

Chapter 10: Exec Meeting

Gary and Randal Present:
- What are the pros and cons of Gary and Randal's Critical Chain proposal?
- Did Grant follow through on his commitment to help Gary and Randal in the Exec meeting (Chapter 8 discussion)? If so, how?

Micky Presents:
- What are the pros and cons of Micky's outsourcing solution?

Epilog:
- Who won at the board meeting? Micky? Gary and Randal?
- What does Tim want to implement next and why?

Basic Answers to Chapter Questions
Chapter 1: Introductions
LivingTV:
1. What happened to LivingTV?
    a. They could not develop the market fast enough. They could not get the new technology out soon enough. They were unable to grow the revenues as quickly as they had expanded the company and counter the resulting growth in expenses.

Tim and Randal Reconnect:
1. What is Critical Chain useful for?
    a. To help deliver projects faster and more reliably.
2. What is TOC useful for?
    a. It is a great set of general problem-solving tools that can be used to look at an organization as a whole, identify areas to focus on, and drive overall improvements.
    b. It can be used help focus teams on any improvement effort from Critical Chain, Scrum, Agile, new technology deployments, and so on.

Appendix

Chapter 2: High-Level Critical Chain Overview

What Is TOC and Critical Chain:

1. What is Critical Chain?

    a. *Critical Chain* is a Theory of Constraints solution that addresses the common problems found in project management so you can better plan, manage, and be more successful with projects.

2. What is TOC?

    a. The *Theory of Constraints (TOC for short)* is a general problem-solving model that can be applied to a variety of environments, but it has one fundamental concept. It focuses on identifying the one constraint that is limiting the system overall. So if you focus improvement efforts on this one area, the whole system will benefit and the bottom line of the organization will improve.

Critical Chain Issues, Benefits, and Sample Results:

1. What are some of the common project-management issues Critical Chain can help address?

    a. Your projects miss critical deadlines and market opportunities.

    b. You cut too many key features to make deadlines.

    c. Your products are not competitive enough (due to slow project turnaround, missing deadlines, cutting key features, etc.).

    d. There is too much resource burn-out and turnover.

    e. You go over budget (due to project overruns).

    f. There are internal projects fights over shared resources.

What are some of the Critical Chain benefits?

    a. On-time delivery of products significantly improves.

    b. You are able to complete projects much faster.

    c. Hidden or misused resource capacity is surfaced.

    d. Your company and products are more competitive.

    e. Your company is more profitable.

Get it Done On Time!

Key Parts of Critical Chain:
1. What are some of the key Critical Chain components that help you get results?
   - Project buffers to better manage task variability [frt 1]
   - Reducing bad multi-tasking to find hidden and misused resource capacity [frt 1]
   - Building schedules (back-to-front) and challenging assumptions [frt 1]
   - Organizational analysis (TOC TP) to better understand the overall project environment (creating the CRT and FRT)

Project Buffers:
1. What do project buffers do?
   a. Help to better manage the variability in all projects.
2. What are some of the issues that can cause project variability?
   a. There is more work involved than originally expected, additional scope and requirements are added, resources are not available, tasks take longer than expected, and project disasters happen that might sink a project.

Multi-Tasking:
1. What does reducing bad multi-tasking give you?
   a. It provides clear priorities, focuses resources on key projects versus spreading them out, and encourages quick hand-offs.
2. Is all multi-tasking bad?
   a. No, if you are working on one task and get blocked, working on a second task is fine. If you are juggling multiple tasks and going back and forth between them is slowing you down, then it is bad.

Appendix

Building Schedules:
1. What does building schedules back-to-front give you?
    a. A better way to call out true dependencies that can also be creatively challenged.

Organizational Analysis:
1. What is the benefit of an organizational analysis?
    a. It provides a way to do a root cause analysis of your organizations issues. From there, you can see which issues the Critical Chain general solution can help you address. But as important, you can also see what other areas you will need to work on. This enables you to develop a complete and overall solution that will significantly improve your organization.

Multiple Methodologies:
1. What can influence the success of implementing a new project-management process even if it is a proven process?
    a. How well the culture supports and adopts the solution
    b. How well the process addresses the organization's problems
2. Can you mix other project-management methodologies with Critical Chain?
    a. You can certainly mix project-management methodologies, but you need to have a solid grounding in the methodologies you are trying to mix. It is really important to first focus on getting your Critical Chain experience then you can look at adding other methods into it.

CRT and FRT:
1. What does Tim's CRT/FRT flowcharts help with?
    a. Tim's chart helps visually map out several of the key components and connections between them for both the current situation as well as the desired situation.

2. Is this something that should be shared with everyone?

   a. Tim's charts can be shared with some key people, but in general they are often too detailed and technical to share with everyone. In these cases you may want to leverage the information from the flowcharts for discussions but not share them directly.

Chapter 3: Factors for Success

Introductions:

1. What was Gary's feeling on how good the Critical Chain methodology was?

   a. The methodology did not seem to work well when they had tried to implement it on their own.

2. What was Tim's thinking on why Gary did not get very good results?

   a. No one was certified in Critical Chain and had no one had prior experience implementing Critical Chain.

Key Characteristics of Successful Implementations:

1. What areas are important for successful implementations? What is the benefit of each area?

   a. A Critical Chain implementation expert who really understands the mechanics of the Critical Chain solution, how to use it correctly to help organizations increase throughput, and how to successfully implement it in an organization.

   b. Someone who has Critical Chain software tool experience.

   c. For complicated and political environments, I personally like to see someone who has a Theory of Constraints Thinking Process background who can do an organizational analysis.

   d. The organization has a compelling need and desire to change.

   e. Setting up the correct metrics.

Appendix

2. If your company is already using Critical Chain, how well do you address the above areas for successful implementations?

    a. *Optional student exercise. Answers vary.*

Environmental Factors:

1. What four organizational issues can be important for successful implementations?

    a. Does the organization's project team take ownership of the Critical Chain solution?

    b. Is senior management brought into the solution?

    c. How complex is your project environment?

    d. Existence of poor project-management practices.

2. What other areas beyond this list do you see as critical for a successful implementation or a potential major issue that could de-rail an implementation?

    a. *Optional student exercise.* Items can include how well a team understands its customers, how well they know the market, how well can they define the product's requirements, etc.

3. If your company is already using Critical Chain, how well do you address the above organizational issues? Are there other issues that are a concern?

    a. *Optional student exercise. Answers vary.*

Chapter 4: How Does the Critical Chain Solution Work

Key Critical Chain Benefits:

1. What are the key Critical Chain benefits?

    a. Project and feeding buffers to better manage variability

    b. Reducing bad multi-tasking to find hidden or misused resource capacity

Get it Done On Time!

    c. Building schedules back-to-front and challenging assumptions

    d. Organizational Analysis (TOC Thinking Process) to better understand the environment

Project and Feeding Buffers, Padding Dates:

1. What does it mean to pad dates? Why can it be problematic?

    a. Padding dates is the practice of adding additional time on top of an engineering deadline. It can be problematic since it can extend the overall project's length and if it is too long this time can get cut by management.

2. What is the management and engineering poker game over?

    a. How much time engineers can get management to add to the schedule to ensure features and quality versus how much time managers can cut from the engineers' estimates to manage costs and hit key market windows.

Project and Feeding Buffers, Project Buffers:

1. What is the value of a project buffer? How is it different than management adding padding (additional time) to the team's deadline?

    a. It provides strategic use of safety time to more effectively protect the overall project's deadline. In doing this, it can help shorten the overall project duration versus padding that just adds additional time.

    b. The project buffer consumption can also be used to trigger planning and response plans if the project starts encountering too many delays.

2. What are some of the behaviors Critical Chain tries to implement to improve project performance? Briefly describe them.

    a. *Roadrunner* refers to the fact that you want resources to start working on a task as soon as it is assigned to them. *Relay race* is that as soon as a task is finished you want them to hand off to the next resource so they can start right away. *Bad multi-tasking* is when resources work on several tasks at once. *Student syndrome* is the temptation to put work off to the last minute.

Appendix

Project and Feeding Buffers, Feeding Buffers
1. What is the value of feeding buffers?
   a. To minimize overall project delays from feeding task issues and delays.

Project and Feeding Buffers, Safety Time:
1. What is safety time?
   a. The extra time (padding) engineers add to a task to protect against delays and paranoia.

Project and Feeding Buffers, Managing Project Variability:
1. What does Critical Chain try to do in regard to variability? How?
   a. Critical Chain sets up ways to manage the variability of a project so companies are less impacted by delays. The feeding buffers minimize delays from feeding paths. Moving safety time out of the tasks and into a project buffer allows you to better protect the project's deadline from delays without adding time. The project behaviors are to help you move as quickly forward in executing the project as you can.

Reducing Bad Multi-Tasking:
1. What does bad multi-tasking do to your deadlines, resource capacity, and responsiveness?
   a. Bad multi-tasking causes deadlines to get stretched out, resource capacity to be wasted, and your responsiveness to be wasted.

Defining the Project Goal and Building Schedules Back-to-Front:
1. What is the first step in building a schedule back-to-front?
   a. The first step is to be sure that you have a clearly defined project goal.
2. What does the phrase *in order to (previous task) we must (successive task)* first help you with?
   a. It allows you to make sure you have captured all of the necessary tasks and dependencies.

3. What does *in order to (goal) we must (and list out the key tasks in the schedule)* allow you to do?

   a. Make sure that you have captured all of the key requirements in the schedule.

4. Overall, how does building the schedule back-to-front help you?

   a. It allows you to make sure you capture key dependencies and tasks that might be overlooked by just listing requirements, it helps you make sure you clearly define the project goal, and it helps you make sure the key tasks you are doing are sufficient to reach that goal.

Organizational Analysis:

1. How does Critical Chain and the organizational analysis work together to provide a more complete solution?

   a. Critical Chain helps address the common project-management issues. The organizational analysis helps you identify organizational issues that could significantly limit the results of your Critical Chain implementation as well as helps you see what needs to help improve the organization as a whole.

2. How does the organizational analysis help?

   a. The organizational analysis helps in getting the organizational buy-in on what problems need to be addressed, how, and why Critical Chain and some other key improvements are necessary.

Chapter 5: Championing Ideas

LivingTV Interactive's Dilemma:

1. What was LivingTV's dilemma? What choice is it struggling with?

   a. In order to expand, LivingTV needed to decide if it wanted to first expand into a nationwide service or expand the number of programs and games it offered.

2. Why was LivingTV stuck?

   a. LivingTV was stuck because it only had the funding to either go nationwide or expand programming; it could not do both.

Appendix

LivingTV Interactive's Conflict Cloud:
1. What is the common goal that both sides share?
    a. Everyone wanted LivingTV to grow and be successful.
2. What are the wants of each side?
    a. One side wanted LivingTV to go nationwide.
    b. One side wanted LivingTV to expand its programming.
3. What are the needs driving the wants of each side?
    a. One side needed to have a market large enough to attract advertising revenue.
    b. One side needed to have enough programming to develop subscriber revenue.

Looking for Possible Resolutions:
1. Of the AB, BD, AC, CD', DD' connections, which three connections in the cloud does Tim try to challenge? Why those three specifically?
    a. DD' to challenge the assumptions behind the conflict itself.
    b. BD and CD' to challenge the assumptions between each side's need and each side's want.

Spark of an Idea:
1. What link (AB, AC, BD, CD', DD') did Tim challenge?
    a. CD'
2. What assumption did he identify that he was able to challenge?
    a. There was no way to get additional programming without paying additional royalties.
3. How did breaking this assumption create a win-win solution for the company?
    a. The "go deep" subscriber/programming side benefited since there were now able to increase the number of programs supported without significant expense by not having to pay royalties to get pre-distribution access to shows.

Get it Done On Time!

b. The side that wanted to "go broad" benefited since they will now have the money and resources to expand.

c. With the pre-show, both sides were able to protect and move forward with their needs.

Initial Manager Meeting:

1. What was Tim trying to prevent by meeting each of the directors before the Exec review?

    a. His idea failing by getting stalled by the company's approval process. In addition, Tim could educate each decision maker about the idea as well as have a chance to address their concerns in advance.

Lobbying in Preparation for the Exec Review:

1. What did John, Mike, Bill, and Jim like about the pre-show concept?

    a. John liked how it supported his goals to expand the number of shows LivingTV supported, the idea's ability to support any show, and the concept gave his team a full week to develop each week's script.

    b. Mike liked that the idea was not technically challenging to implement.

    c. Jim liked that it gave the opportunity to produce any and as many shows as LivingTV wanted without the high cost of royalties.

2. What were John, Mike, Bill, and Jim's reservations about the pre-show concept?

    a. Everyone had concerns around the legality of the developing LivingTV content based on TV shows that have been broadcast.

    b. Mike wanted Tim to review the idea with Peter in case there were additional technical concerns.

    c. Jim had concerns around legal and maintaining the company's relationship with broadcasters.

3. How did their responses relate to each of their respective departments?

    a. John focused on programming operations questions, Mike on engineering and technical questions, and Jim on executive and strategic relationship questions.

Appendix

4. When pitching an idea, how would your approach change based on your audience?
   a. Everyone needs a general idea of the solution, but each person's interest and questions often focus on where they are in the organization (i.e., John in operations, Mike in technical, and Jim in strategic).

The Exec Review:

1. How did Tim and Lori's work help in the Exec review?
   a. At the start of the meeting, everyone already understood the concept and Tim and Lori had been able to understand and help address the majority of concerns. This streamlined the meeting.

Chapter 6: Single Project Implementation Steps

Phoenix Setup:

1. What are two ways to implement Critical Chain into an organization? Which one is more ideal than the other?
   - When looking at moving an organization onto Critical Chain ideally, you should try to move the whole organization. If time is an issue, then you can look at staggering the implementation and pick one or two high-impact projects to focus on. They need to have a bottom-line impact as well and cannot be side projects since the effort needed and results created would not be taken seriously.

2. Is it possible to intercept a project that is already in flight with Critical Chain?
   - If necessary it is possible to intercept a project already in process and simply build the new Critical Chain schedule from where the project is currently at to the end.

3. To really make a culture change in an organization, what three things do you need?
   - Top management buy-in and agreement to lead the charge.
   - Determination of key measurement changes that will incentivize the desired behaviors of the new culture.
   - Education for all involved, including the new measurements. (Bibliography 1)

Phoenix Network Build:

1. As part of the network build, does all of the team need to know the Critical Chain concepts?

    - As part of the network build, it is important that the managers and the team learns the key Critical Chain concepts [Chapters 2 and 4 items]

2. What defines the end of the project?

    - You want to be sure to build the project to throughput (where you generate income).

3. What phrasing can you use when building out the schedule and checking dependencies?

    - You look at the project's goal and build backward using the phrasing *in order to.. we must..* and add in any dependencies.

4. What is BORA and what is it used for?

    - When you need to compress and tighten a schedule up, you can look at BORA: *B*reak a link, *O*verlap tasks, *R*educe scope or duration, or *A*dd a resource.

5. What are some of the issues Tim, Gary, and Jeremy run into when building out the Phoenix schedule?

    - Jeremy wants to be sure Gary has signed off on replanning the Phoenix schedule using a new methodology.
    - They need to build the schedule to throughput, so when the customer actually approves the features and revenues are generated.
    - Critical Chain is staggering the tasks based on resource availability.
    - Tasks are assigned to the manager's name as opposed to the resource's name.
    - Jeremy added padding back into some of the focus times for some of the tasks.
    - The schedule is too long and the team needs to use BORA to tighten it up.

Appendix

Phoenix Execution:

1. How often should the team update the schedule?
   a. The team should have regular, typically weekly, schedule updates.
2. What does the fever chart measure?
   a. The fever chart measures how much buffer you have consumed compared to how much of the project you have completed.
3. What do the different colors of the fever chart mean?
   a. Green means you are on track, yellow means you are falling behind and need to look at ways to recover, and red means that you are putting the project deadline at risk and need to act to add time back into the buffer.
4. How can you recover time?
   a. To recover time, review BORA: Break a link, Overlap tasks, Reduce scope or duration, or Add a resource.
5. What are some of the key behaviors that you want during project execution? See Chapters 2 and 4 for more details.
   a. Roadrunner: You encourage people to work as quickly as they can.
   b. Relay race: You encourage people to hand off work to the next resource (dependency) as quickly as possible.
   c. Reduce bad multi-tasking: You want to avoid any multi-tasking that stretches out work and delays hand-offs.
   d. Do not beat up resources for missing focused times; they are aggressive by design so you should expect that several will be missed. You'll want to manage the overall project buffer and overall deadline, not micro-manage resources.

Phoenix Post-Mortem Plan:

1. What is POOGI and what is it for?
   - POOGI stands for the Process Of OnGoing Improvement. Once you have set up a new process, you need to maintain and continue to improve upon it.

Micky's Urgent Requests:

1. What is the value of a change control process?
   - Even when you set up Critical Chain (or any system) it is not foolproof. If you let too much work into the system, you will flood it. So you must have good discipline and manage a good change control process.
2. If you know you will always have changes at key points in the schedule, what are some of the possible options?
   - Look at trying to minimize these changes (i.e. change control) as well as proactively reserve capacity for these changes.

Chapter 7: Ambitious Targets

Background and QA Issues:

1. What is the challenge faced by the QA team?
   a. The engineering schedule ran late and the overall project deadline held so the QA timeframe was severely compressed with the expectation that the team would hold to the original quality and testing guidelines.

Define Your Goal:

1. What criteria makes up a clear goal?
   a. It's clear, measurable, and has specific criteria and dates.

List Out Clear Issues and Their Impact:

1. What issues are impacting QA?
   a. Software is often late, software's delays reduces the time left for QA, software going into test is of poor quality, QA is blamed for software's low quality, and software engineers change requirements without informing QA.

Appendix

Define Intermediate Objects (IOs):

1. Who should be first to make suggestions to address an issue raised? Why?

    a. The person who first raised the issue should have the first opportunity to make a suggestion. Afterward, others can add their own suggestions as it makes sense.

2. What are "flying pig" suggestions and why are they useful?

    a. Flying pig suggestions are "way out there" suggestions that initially seem impossible, such as we can breathe under water, we can land on the moon, we all become rich, etc. They are useful in that they give you a direction as long as you can eventually come back and convert the flying pig idea back into something realistic and implementable.

3. At the end, Tim checks the suggestions that Nir and Anthony came up with against the goal. Why?

    a. Tim is doing a quick check to make sure that there were not any other major issues that would prevent the team from reaching the goal that had not been discussed.

Sequence the Intermediate Objectives (IOs):

1. What three things is Tim looking for from each suggestion?

    a. Sequencing, owner, timeline.

        i. Sequencing: Can this be done in parallel with other tasks or is it dependent on another task finishing first?

        ii. Owner: Who owns completing this task?

        iii. Timeline: When do you expect them to finish the task? Will you have several status checkpoints to review progress?

2. What do ambitious targets allow you to do over a task-oriented schedule?

    a. Focus on putting together an overall plan that includes not only the traditional tasks needed to complete a schedule, but also a plan that captures the issues you are concerned about and your plans on how to overcome these concerns.

Get it Done On Time! | 179

3. What are the high-level steps in building an Ambitious Target?
    a. Develop a goal
    b. Identify issues
    c. Develop suggestions
    d. Sequence the suggestions

Chapter 8: Individual Buy-In

Meeting with Sales and Marketing:

1. What does Tim learn in talking with Ashley?
    a. Missed dates and features have caused the company to incur penalties, get less desirable contract terms, and lose future contracts.
    b. The company is missing revenue targets.
    c. Several of the execs have lost trust in engineering's ability to deliver.
    d. Micky has once looked into adding additional product lines [crt 30].
    e. Competitors are catching up and getting contracts the company once had.

Meeting with Human Resources:

1. What does Tim learn in talking with Herb?
    a. The company has lost several good people due to tight deadlines, priorities switching, and unrealistic schedules.
    b. Competitors are ramping up and picking up some of the people who left and that in turn has lead to poaching of additional employees.
    c. Micky had asked the execs to look at a potential 10% resource cut across the company, but is unlikely to follow through on it since it would have long-term consequences.

Appendix

Randal and Tim Prep for the Meeting with Grant:

1. What are the six layers of resistance used for?
   a. To help get buy-in in an effective and systematic way, help address people's concerns, and help them understand and ideally agree to your proposal.
2. What are the six layers of resistance?
   a. Layer 1: Lack of consensus on the problem.
   b. Layer 2: People do not agree on the direction of the solution.
   c. Layer 3: Arguing the proposed solution cannot yield the desired outcome.
   d. Layer 4: Yes, but. Concerns about potential negative side-effects from proposed solution.
   e. Layer 5: Obstacles that stand in the way of implementing solution into the environment.
   f. Layer 6: Raising doubts, wait and see, unverbalized fears.
3. What TOC tools are used for the first four layers?
   a. Layer 1: Lack of consensus on the problem. CRT tool.
   b. Layer 2: People do not agree on the direction of the solution. Cloud and Injection tool.
   c. Layer 3: Arguing the proposed solution cannot yield the desired outcome. FRT tool.
   d. Layer 4: Yes, but. Concerns about potential side-effects from proposed solution. Negative Branch (NBR) tool.
4. Why is it bad to show the CRT/FRT and use TOC terminology when trying to get buy-in from someone not familiar with TOC?
   a. When you start showing CRTs and FRTs and start using TOC lingo on people who are not familiar with TOC, instead of them being amazed by your insights, they in fact will be turned off by the complexity and your arrogance in assuming they would understand something so new and different instantly.

Get it Done On Time!

5. Why is it important to blame the system?
   a. You want to focus attention on the system, not go around finger pointing and blaming people.
   b. It is not that any one person or group is trying to undermine the company. The system, the way you operate, is holding you back. The CRT outlines this system and how it is interconnected. Companies need to focus their efforts on understanding, blaming, and changing the system.

6. Why bother with the organizational analysis, CRT, FRT, and getting all of the execs' to buy-in? Wouldn't it just be simpler to build the Critical Chain schedules, add the buffers, and implement it in engineering without the rest of the organization's involvement?
   a. It could work briefly. But in the long run it would likely fall apart. As noted in the factors for success [Chapter 3], the organizational buy-in is needed. If management is not brought in and understand the project buffers they will just cut them and that will undermine Critical Chain's success. With the cut project buffers, you are more likely to miss deadlines and in turn management will push even more to switch to some other methodology du jour. The same is true with the buffer management and project behaviors. Without management support, they will not work and in turn the Critical Chain solution will not work.

7. Why is it so important to close the deal?
   a. You are holding a meeting for a reason. If you present everything, but do not close it with a confirmed call to action, then people are informed but nothing changes. You need the call to action to get ensure that you get some level of commitment and cause change.

Meeting with Grant:

1. What major stages does Tim go through in talking with Grant?
   a. Quantify the issues (Layer 1)
   b. Explain the core conflict and key injection (Layer 2)
   c. Walk through the vision/FRT (Layer 3)
   d. Close the deal

Appendix

2. What areas does Tim go through when he walks through the vision (Layer 2) with Grant?
   a. Throughput
   b. Project buffers and behaviors
   c. Organizational analysis
   d. Summarize the vision
3. What does Tim learn in talking to Grant?
   a. About 40% of the projects have some delays.
   b. He and Gary have to juggle project priorities between proprietary features and infrastructure versus general features and infrastructure.
   c. Micky states the revenues from contracts are down 30%.

Chapter 9: Almost

Randal and Tim Prep:
1. What does Tim choose to focus on for his meeting with Micky compared to his meeting with Grant?
   a. Tim is catering to the audience. Grant lives a lot of the engineering issues, so it made sense to start the discussion there. Micky is the CEO and sees and lives the company's struggles so starting with the cloud of the company's conflict should work well for him.

Tim Meets with Micky:
1. What three steps does Tim go through when presenting to Micky?
   a. Show the cloud
   b. Blame the system and highlight key issues from the CRT
   c. Introduce the key injection and vision
2. Would you have done anything different in meeting with Micky?
   a. *Optional student exercise. Answers vary.*

Get it Done On Time! | 183

Next Steps:

1. What are some of the benefits Randal and Gary are seeing from implementing Critical Chain on the Phoenix project?

    a. They hit a number of issues and consumed some of the project buffer, but are still on track to hit their deliverables.

    b. The development team feels more confident that the schedule is realistic and they actually have a chance to succeed.

    c. Randal has been working with Gary to talk with the customers to better enable a clean feature checkout. The customers appreciate the attention and Gary feels it will help them get payments a month early if the schedules continue to hold up.

Chapter 10: Exec Meeting

Gary and Randal Present:

1. What are the pros and cons of Gary and Randal's Critical Chain proposal?

Pros:

- Phoenix is on track to generate better revenues than with past projects (no excessive overtime, no customer penalties for incomplete features).

- Phoenix is on track to generate revenues earlier than with past projects.

- The techniques used can be carried over to other projects and, in turn, help them bring in better revenues sooner.

- Keeping development in internal will protect their intellectual property.

Cons:

- Engineering has a long history of missing deadlines.

- Engineering has a long history of promising to improve with limited success.

- Engineering needs time to fully implement this new process across the company's various projects.

2. Did Grant follow through on his commitment to help Gary and Randal in the Exec meeting (Chapter 8 discussion)? If so, how?
   - Yes, Grant followed through on his commitment. Grant shared his belief that Critical Chain would help the organization move forward and would help them turn things around.

Micky Presents:
   - What are the pros and cons of Micky's outsourcing solution?

Pros:
   - Development can be done at a fraction of the cost.
   - They can use freed up funds to aggressively market and expand product offerings.
   - Development can be done by a company with a history of delivering on time.
   - They can transition to the outsourcing company quickly (in theory).
   - They can add development capacity by expanding their contract.

Cons:
   - How quickly the outsourcing company can actually ramp up needs further investigation.
   - They are entrusting their intellectual property to an outside organization.
   - They lay off a significant number of their existing staff.
   - They assume the outsourcing company can innovate as well as the existing teams that have had years to ramp up.
   - They assume the outsourcing company will not significantly increase its fees.

Epilog:
1. Who won at the board meeting? Micky? Gary and Randal?
   - The company won overall by getting a solution that would help it succeed. Gary and Randal were able to preserve the local development team based on the early success they were able to get using Critical Chain on the Phoenix project as well as set the development team up for continued success. Micky was able to cement his leadership role as the new co-CEO.
2. What does Tim want to implement next and why?
   - After implementing single project Critical Chain to help each project do well, he wants to look at Critical Chain multi-project to help the organization manage multiple parallel projects effectively.

TOC Resources

To learn the latest information and more about TOC, TOC solutions including Critical Chain, and TOC conferences, results, and testimonials, consider the following:

- The Goldratt Institute (www.goldratt.com); the birthplace of TOC
- The Theory of Constraints International Certification Organization (www.tocico.org); TOC Training and Certification Organization
- Googling your favorite topic

Bibliography

Chapter 2: High-Level Critical Chain Overview

- Goldratt Success: "AGI Results" [Online]. Available at www.goldratt.com, November 13, 2010.
- Goldratt Marketing Success [Online]. Available at www.toc-goldratt.com, November 13, 2010.

- Realization Success [Online]. Available at www.realization.com, November 13, 2010.
- Prochain Success: "Prochain Results." [Online] Available at www.prochain.com/clients/results.html, November 13, 2010.
- "Using Critical Chain to break the World Sped Record for Building a House," [Online]. Available at www.toc-goldratt.com/tocweekly/2013/05/using-critical-chain-to-break-the-world-speed-record-for-building-a-house/, January 20, 2016.

Chapter 4: How Does the Critical Chain Solution Work?

- Goldratt, Eliyahu M. *Critical Chain,* North River Press, 2002.
- Wikipedia. "Critical Chain." [Online]. Available at www.en.wikipedia.org/wiki/Critical_chain_project_management, December 23, 2014.
- Avraham Y Goldratt Institute. "A White Paper: Theory of Constraints Project Management—A Brief Introduction to the Basics." Available from AGI December 13, 2010.

Chapter 5: Championing Ideas

- Avraham Y Goldratt Institute, "Management Skills Course: Conflict Resolution," 1993.
- Wikipedia. "Evaporating Cloud." [Online]. Available at http://en.wikipedia.org/wiki/Core_Conflict_Cloud, December 23, 2010.

Chapter 6: Implementation Steps

- Bibliography 1 interview with Suzan Bergland, January, 2016.
- Bibliography 2 interview with Tina Merry, October, 2006.

Chapter 7: Ambitious Targets
- Avraham Y Goldratt Institute, "Management Skills Course: Ambitious Targets," 1993.

Chapter 8: Individual Buy-In
- Interview with Suzan Bergland, January, 2016

Basic Answers to Chapter Questions
Chapter 2
- Wikipedia. "Critical Chain." [Online]. Available at https://en.wikipedia.org/wiki/Critical_chain_project_management, April 3, 2016.
- Wikipedia. "Theory of Constraints." [Online]. Available at https://en.wikipedia.org/wiki/Theory_of_constraints, April 3, 2016.

Index

A

Ambitious targets
    background and QA issues, 177
    key steps, 152
    questions, 161
Avraham Goldratt Institute (AGI), 10

B

Bad multi-tasking, 41, 165, 170
    reduces, 46
    tasks and projects, 48–51
Bibliography, 185, 187
Board room meeting, 135
    epilog, 141
    exec meeting, 183, 185
    exec review, 155
    Gray approaches, 136
    Micky presentation, 138
    Randal presentaion, 136
    review, 140
Building schedules, 166
Building schedules back-to-front, 170

C, D

Clear
    definition, 95
    issues and impacts, 95
Concise definition, 95
Critical Chain
    AGI, 10
    answers, 164
    benefits, 9, 38, 146, 168
    building schedules
        back-to-front, 51, 53–54, 56
    CCPM benefits, 148
    common project management
        issues, 8
    components, 146
    Goldratt's marketing group, 11
    high level mechanics, 12
    issues, 145
    managing variability, 6
    multiple project management
        methodologies, 18
    problem-solving model, 7
    ProChain, 11
    project and feeding buffers
        bad multi-tasking, 46, 48
        feeding buffer, 42
        highway analogy, 46
        padding dates, 39
        project buffers, 39–40
        project variability management, 45
        safety time, 43
    project buffers
        aggressive task estimates, 14
        bad multi-tasking, 15
        building schedules
            (back to front), 16–17
        focused time, 14
        manage variability, 12
        organizational analysis, 17
        safety time, 14
    project management issues, 7
    questions, 156–157
    realization, 11
    resources, 6
    results, 10, 12
    TOC solution, 6, 145
    velocity, 18
    web sites, 146
    wrapping up, 18

© Eric Bergland 2016
E. Bergland, *Get it Done On Time!*, DOI 10.1007/978-1-4842-1860-0

Index

Current Reality Tree (CRT), 19–21
    LivingTV Interactive
        cloud captures, 72
        core confilct, 71
        CRT diagram, 73–74
    meeting peoples, 122, 124
    Phoenix project, 89–90

E

Environmental factors
    organizational issues, 33
    overview, 32
    Randal implementation, 34
    roles and responsibilities, 34
    solution and implementation, 34

F

Feeding buffers, 42–43, 169
Future Reality Tree (FRT)
    board room meeting, 143–144
    Critical Chain, 21–23
    Intermediate Objectives (IOs), 105
    LivingTV Interactive, 69–70
    meeting peoples, 122–125, 127
    Phoenix project, 90–92
    successful implementations, 35–36

G

Gary
    presentation, 136
    questions, 162
Grant, 117
    approaches, 136
    core conflict and key injection, 118
    FRT, 119
        organizational analysis, 120
        project buffers and behaviors, 120
        synopsis, 121
        Throughput, 119
    issue, 118
    review, 122

H

High-level implementation, 77–78
    Micky, requests, 151

Phoenix
    execution, 150
    network build, 150
    Post-Mortem plan, 151
    setup, 149
    questions, 160
Human resources (HR), 110–111

I, J, K

Individual buy-in
    approaches, 153–154
    key steps, 152
    layers, 152
    questions, 161
Intermediate Objectives (IOs), 178
    concatenation, 101, 103–104
    definition, 96, 98–100
    results, 104–105

L

LivingTV Interactive
    answers, 163
    assumptions, 149
    background, 58
    conflict cloud, 59, 172
    Critical Chain, 145
    dilemma, 59, 171
    direct conflict, 60
    exec review, 64–67, 173–174
    history, 1
    idea, 148
    initial manager meeting, 63, 173
    Peter meeting, 66
    questions, 155, 158–159
    Randal reconnection, 2
    realtime ideas, 61
    resolutions, 60, 172
    stuck, 59
    Tim and Randal, 68
    Tim reconnection, 2
    TOC, 2, 145, 149

M

Measurable goal definition, 95
Meeting peoples, 129

Index

CRT/FRT issues, 180
Grant, 180–181 (see also Grant)
human resources, 110–111, 179
layers, 180
meeting preparation, 112, 114–115, 117
Micky, 130
    cloud, 130
    CRT issues, 131
    injection and vision, 131–132
    steps, 132–133
sales and marketing, 108–110, 179
TOC tools, 180
Methodologies, 166
Micky, 87–88, 130
    cloud, 130
    CRT issues, 131
    injection and vision, 131–132
    presentation, 138
    requests, 151
    steps, 132–133

N

Negative branch (NBR), 154

O

Organizational analysis, 56, 148, 166, 171

P, Q

Padding dates, 39, 169
Phoenix project
    execution, 84–86, 150
    Micky, 88
    network build, 79–82, 84, 150
    post-mortem plan, 86, 151
    setup, 149
ProChain, 11
Project buffers, 40, 165, 169
Project implementation, 174–176

R

Randal
    and Tim preparation, 182
    and Tim presentation, 155
    Micky, 182
    presentation, 136
    questions, 162
Relay race, 41
Roadrunner, 41, 169

S

Sales and marketing director, 108–110
Student syndrome, 41
Successful implementations
    characteristics, 27, 167
    Critical Chain Implementation expert, 27–28
    environmental factors, 168
    environmental issues, 147
    experience, 28
    factors, 25–26, 147 (see also Environmental factors)
    organization needs
        compelling reason, 30
        Randal and Gary, 30
        Tim, 30
        TOC thinking processes, 30
    questions, 157
    software tool experience, 28
    metrics, 31
    TOC TP thinking process background, 29

T, U, V, W, X, Y, Z

Theory of Constraints Thinking Process (TOC TP), 18, 29
Theory of Constraints (TOC), 2–3
    key concepts, 145
    resources, 185

Get the eBook for only $5!

Why limit yourself?

Now you can take the weightless companion with you wherever you go and access your content on your PC, phone, tablet, or reader.

Since you've purchased this print book, we're happy to offer you the eBook in all 3 formats for just $5.

Convenient and fully searchable, the PDF version enables you to easily find and copy code—or perform examples by quickly toggling between instructions and applications. The MOBI format is ideal for your Kindle, while the ePUB can be utilized on a variety of mobile devices.

To learn more, go to www.apress.com/companion or contact support@apress.com.

All Apress eBooks are subject to copyright. All rights are reserved by the Publisher, whether the whole or part of the material is concerned, specifically the rights of translation, reprinting, reuse of illustrations, recitation, broadcasting, reproduction on microfilms or in any other physical way, and transmission or information storage and retrieval, electronic adaptation, computer software, or by similar or dissimilar methodology now known or hereafter developed. Exempted from this legal reservation are brief excerpts in connection with reviews or scholarly analysis or material supplied specifically for the purpose of being entered and executed on a computer system, for exclusive use by the purchaser of the work. Duplication of this publication or parts thereof is permitted only under the provisions of the Copyright Law of the Publisher's location, in its current version, and permission for use must always be obtained from Springer. Permissions for use may be obtained through RightsLink at the Copyright Clearance Center. Violations are liable to prosecution under the respective Copyright Law.

The manufacturer's authorised representative in the EU is Springer Nature Customer Service Centre GmbH, Europaplatz 3, 69115 Heidelberg, Germany. If you have any concerns regarding our products, please contact ProductSafety@springernature.com

Printed and bound by CPI Group (UK) Ltd, Croydon, CR0 4YY

25/03/2026

02078172-0010